MODERN CRUISE SHIPS, 1965-1990

A Photographic Record

William H. Miller, Jr.

DOVER PUBLICATIONS, INC., New York

For FRANK DUFFY

dear friend, fellow author,
man-about-the-harbor

Copyright © 1992 by William H. Miller, Jr.
All rights reserved under Pan American and International Copyright Conventions.

Published in Canada by General Publishing Company, Ltd., 30 Lesmill Road, Don Mills, Toronto, Ontario.
Published in the United Kingdom by Constable and Company, Ltd., 3 The Lanchesters, 162–164 Fulham Palace Road, London W6 9ER.

Modern Cruise Ships, 1965–1990: A Photographic Record is a new work, first published by Dover Publications, Inc., in 1992.

Manufactured in the United States of America
Dover Publications, Inc.
31 East 2nd Street
Mineola, N.Y. 11501

Library of Congress Cataloging-in-Publication Data

Miller, William H., 1948–
    Modern cruise ships, 1965–1990 : a photographic record / by William H. Miller, Jr.
        p.   cm.
    Includes index.
    ISBN 0-486-26753-9 (pbk.)
    1. Cruise ships—Pictorial works. 2. Ocean travel—Pictorial works.   I. Title.
VM381.M4497   1991
387.2'43'0222—dc20   91-23184
                                                                                                      CIP

Acknowledgments

Many hands have assisted in assembling this pictorial parade. The author wishes to make known his very special thanks to Goran Damstrom, Frank Duffy, Alan Liddy, Ove Nielsen, Hisashi Noma, Antonio Scrimali, Raimondo Starcevich, Willie Tinnemeyer, Everett Viez and Steffen Weirauch. These individuals have shown exceptional support, kindness and encouragement.

Other forms of assistance, pieces of information and kind cooperation came from: Susan Alpert, Captain Eric Ashton-Irvine, Julie Benson, Philippe Brebant, Michael Cassar, James Ciani, Luis Miguel Correia, Pamela Cunningham, Alex Duncan, Kathleen Dunlap, Arnold Egeland, Jennifer Foley de la Cruz, Peter Fraser, Yoshi Fukawa, Max Hall, F. Leonard Jackson, Eric Johnson, Wolfgang Kaehler, Jan Loeff, Dean Miller, Chris Montegriffo, Bert Novelli, Fred Rodriguez, Selim San, James Shaw, Roger Sherlock, Richard Steck, Bob Wands and Joseph Wilhelm. Companies and other organizations that assisted include: American President Lines, Backus Aerial Photography, Inc., Carnival Cruise Lines, Clipper Line, Crystal Cruises, Cunard Line, Delta Queen Steamboat Co., Exploration Cruise Lines, Flying Camera, Inc., Grace Line, Hapag-Lloyd, Hapag-Lloyd Shipyards, Holland-America Line, Kloster Group, Lloydwerft Shipyards, Matson Line, Moran Towing & Transportation Co., P & O Lines, Port Authority of New York & New Jersey, Port of Le Havre Authority, Port of Miami, Port of Vancouver, Princess Cruises, Royal Admiral Cruises, Royal Caribbean Cruise Lines, Royal Viking Line, Seabourn Cruise Lines, Schiffsfoto Jansen, Sitmar Cruises, Society Expeditions, South China Morning Post, Ltd., Southern Newspapers, Ltd., Sun Line, U.S. Coast Guard, Wärtsilä Marine Shipyards and Windstar Sail Cruises.

And, of course, my deepest appreciation to my family, to Abe Michaelson and to the staff at Dover Publications.

Sources and Photographers

American President Lines Archives: 19 (top).
Backus Aerial Photography, Inc.: 103 (top).
Bahamas News Bureau: 20 (bottom).
Bermuda News Bureau: 8, 33.
Philippe Brebant Collection: 7 (top), 55 (bottom).
British Columbia Port Authority: 127 (bottom).
Carnival Cruise Lines: 48, 95–97, 126.
Michael Cassar: 51, 60 (bottom), 61 (top), 62 (top & middle), 102 (bottom).
James Ciani: 5.
Clipper Line: 28.
Luis Miguel Correia: 56.
Crystal Cruises: 112 (bottom), 124 (bottom).
Cunard Line: 34–37.
Pamela Cunningham: 57 (bottom).
Delta Queen Steamboat Company: 72/73.
Francis J. Duffy: 104, 123, 124 (top), 177, 178.
Alex Duncan: 63 (bottom), 69 (top).
Arnold S. Egeland Collection: 38, 39 (top).
Exploration Cruise Lines: 100.
Flying Camera, Inc.: 9, 10, 14, 15, 26 (top), 31, 32 (top), 41 (top), 79, 85, 86, 99, 114 (top), 116 (bottom), 127 (top).
Yoshi Fukawa: 101.
German-Atlantic Line: 32 (bottom).
Grace Line: 16, 17.
Jack Grove/Society Expedition: 71 (top).
Hapag-Lloyd: 84.
Hapag-Lloyd Shipyards: 77, 78, 80/81, 103 (bottom).
Holland America Cruises: 43 (top).
Holland-America Line: 11, 43 (bottom), 44 (bottom), 45 (top & middle), 87, 88, 114, 115.
M. Ichiei, 101.
Eric Ashton Irvine Collection: 4.
F. Leonard Jackson: 24, 26 (bottom).
Eric Johnson: 65 (top).
Wolfgang Kaehler/Society Expeditions: 71 (bottom).
Kloster Group: 116 (top).
P. A. Kroehnert: 69 (middle & bottom), 78 (right), 80/81, 103 (bottom).
Lloydwerft: 69 (middle & bottom).

Matson Lines: 19 (bottom).
A. Molinari: 117.
Montegriffo, Chris: 23.
Moran Towing & Transportation Company: 12, 13.
News Events Photo Service Inc.: 115.
Ove Nielsen: 55 (top), 67 (top), 68, 94 (top).
P & O Lines: 22, 25 (top).
Palmer Pictures: 19 (top).
Port Authority of New York & New Jersey: 30, 44 (top), 98.
Port of Le Havre Authority: 64.
Port of Miami: 128/129.
Princess Cruises: 42, 92, 93 (top), 112 (top, left), 118/119.
J. Fred Rodriguez: 7 (bottom), 8, 21, 25 (bottom).
Royal Admiral Cruises: 62 (bottom), 63.
Royal Caribbean Cruise Lines; 82, 106–111.
Royal Cruise Line: 60 (top).
Royal Viking Line: 40, 41 (bottom).
Selim San: 75 (middle).
Schiffsfotos Jansen: 54.
Antonio Scrimali: 53, 61 (bottom), 75 (bottom), 117.
Seabourn Cruise Lines: 112 (top, right), 120, 121.
James L. Shaw: 6, 62 (bottom).
Roger Sherlock: 18.
Sitmar Cruises: 46/47, 89.
Society Expeditions: 71.
South China Morning Post, Ltd.: 74.
Southern Newspapers, Ltd.: 90 (bottom).
Raimondo Starcevich: 52 (top), 65 (bottom).
Sun Line: 58, 59.
Willie Tinnemeyer Collection: 17, 20, 43 (bottom), 44 (bottom), 45, 49 (top).
U.S. Coast Guard: 2/3, 45 (bottom).
Everett E. Viez Collection: 2/3, 33.
Bob Wands: 49 (bottom).
Wärtsilä Shipyards: 39 (bottom), 40, 80, 83, 90 (top), 91, 93 (bottom), 94 (bottom).
Steffen Weirauch Collection: 27, 52 (bottom), 57 (top), 66, 67 (bottom), 70, 75 (top & middle), 102 (top), 113.
Windstar Sail Cruises: 125.

Contents

Foreword

"YOU WILL NEVER forget your first cruise," they say. My first seagoing experience was as a teenager on board the British India Line school ship *Dunera*. Coming from the center of England, I had never been on a ship, yet alone sailed on one. I remember with fond memory those first steps ashore in foreign lands—Vigo, Cadiz and Lisbon—but perhaps more so those aromatic shipboard sensations—fresh-baked bread near the galley and, just yards away, the sweet smell of diesel fuel and lubricating oil wafting up from the engine room. I remember the gentle vibration and the hum of the ventilation; long, painted corridors; heavy steel doors; round portholes with the sea rushing past just feet away; shining linoleum; polished brass; and those dormitories with 30 steel bunks, quiet till all the boys came back from shore to cause minor mayhem. The Master at Arms peers in and suddenly all is quiet—except for the ship. Ships—living, breathing, moving. Machinery to some; almost human to me.

These initial experiences influenced my choice of career. I was to spend 12 months on the old training ship *Worcester*, still floating on the Thames in 1970 and over 60 years old, before I sailed away as a deck cadet on the general cargo ship *Clan Malcolm*. In the early seventies, the British and Commonwealth fleet still had seven passenger ships, the "lavender hull mob" of Union Castle Line, and when I first qualified I was attached to *Reina del Mar* as third officer. In those days Miami was just the last stop on the way down to the Florida Keys made famous by Hemingway.

Cruising was mainly a British affair, still thought of as a pastime of the wealthy, the retired and the Blackpool landladies on their annual vacation. The heyday of the liner service was over and younger ships were refitted for the two-week sojourn to Norway and the Mediterranean in summer, the Caribbean in spring and autumn, and even further afield in winter.

Shaw Savill and the P & O went to Australia; we went to South Africa. For three months of the year, *Reina del Mar* cruised to South America from Cape Town, ten days across the South Atlantic, ten days on the coast in Rio, Santos, Buenos Aires and Montevideo, then back. Now that's what I call cruising—long, relaxing days at sea, warm, quiet nights. No telex, no fax, no T.V., just a growing anticipation for ports to come. I was to do the same trip ten years later on the *QE2* at twice the speed. It wasn't quite the same.

I was particularly pleased to see the *Reina* in Bill's book, bringing back happy memories of my early professional years on a cruise ship different from the ones of today.

These days, of course, our lifestyle is somewhat different from that of twenty years ago; in general, the ships carry more passengers, our crew comes from all over the world (which means training lectures and exercises take more of our time), passengers expect more in the way of food, accommodation, entertainment and itinerary. Spending ten-day periods at sea is unheard of, more usual is seven ports in seven days. In fact, on my present vessel we only have one day at sea in two weeks, and the passengers love it. They spend the day ashore on tour or on the beach, coming back to the ship so exhausted that the nightclub is empty by midnight and after two weeks they need to go home for a rest.

In this book Bill gives us the cruise ships of my era, from the early beginning of the U.S. cruise boom to today, with the large vessels that dwarf the liners of yesteryear. Look at the difference in appearance—no more the long, sweeping bow and cruiser stern, the graceful Italian liners and the purposeful Atlantic leviathans; now we have the stubby fo'c'sle and transom stern and, in between, a shapely variety of boxes with balconies.

As I write, I have before me a picture of the *Crystal Harmony*, Japan's entry into the big-ship cruise market and the latest in a plethora of new buildings that will be competing for American and European passengers. And yet, as the president of Nippon Yusen Kaisha (NYK), the owners of Crystal Cruises, admits, "*Queen Elizabeth 2* is the most famous cruise ship in the world," a title for which he intends to wrestle. Perhaps because *QE2* was the first of the modern era, or the last of the great Atlantic liners, I still think it the most elegant ship. But then, I would be just a little biased, having spent ten years of my life on board.

The long veranda decks have gone, along with the linoleum and the swinging bunks. Now passengers can expect plush carpets, atriums and waterfalls, and multi-channel T.V. in every room, production shows in the lounges, Jacuzzis and fitness centers.

For myself, as I gradually aspire toward command, I look forward to the ships of the future. Already I see that a large hotel chain is building an 18,400-ton vessel based on the SWATH principle (Small Waterplane Area, Twin Hull). This unusual-looking ship has two submarine pontoons, two struts and a bridge platform based on semi-submersible-craft technology. Like a giant catamaran, the passenger spaces will be suspended between the two pontoons and the designers claim the ship will have "superior seaworthiness, stability and minimal vibration." Along with all the other conveniences now expected of today's luxury cruiser, a hydraulically operated floating marina will be located at the stern, acting as a pontoon for water-sport activities.

Whatever the ship becomes, the ocean will still be there in all its moods, and I hope the new liners will not distance the first-time passenger from the romance of the sea. The moonlit nights, with the trade winds blowing, will remain in the memory long after the home movies have been forgotten.

Behind every picture in this book there are memories for thousands of people—of ships, of passengers, of experiences.

Bill, I thank you.

PHIL RENTELL
Chief Officer, *Cunard Countess*
June 1990

Preface

THERE IS ABSOLUTELY nothing like a cruise—it is the best vacation on earth. I have taken about a hundred of them (two-thirds in the capacity of guest lecturer or journalist), but I think of each one as a separate memorable occasion. I can still feel the salt spray, hear the sounds of the whistles, see that fiery sunset off a tropic port. I can still feel that special excitement of departure, when the ship inches away from the pier and severs her link with shore. She is independent, a separate entity unto herself— the floating city, the resort gone to sea.

Late night at sea is also exceptional: wind across the top decks, the darkened funnel, the faint murmurs of blowers and motors and, high above, what seems to be tens of thousands of twinkling stars. And then there is early morning arrival at an exotic port: the greeting of the pilot boat, the shoreline caught in a distant haze and then that tender, cautious moment as the ship is docked. The vendors along the pierside leave an impression, as do the narrators with their detailed commentaries on shore excursions to cathedrals and caves, museums and mountaintops. Finally there is that welcome return to the ship, which has become "home," following a day ashore.

The cruise ships themselves have gone through extraordinary changes over the past quarter century. The days of the wood-paneled *Caronia* and that earlier *Nieuw Amsterdam*, with her Morocco-leather ceiling and Murano chandeliers, and the *France*, with her flawless food, have given way to a generation of white wedding cake cruise ships with names like *Star Princess, Horizon* and *Fantasy*. These successors to that earlier breed are intended to offer the last words in casinos or fitness centers or shopping arcades. A five-deck-high atrium goes to six decks and the record of 150 one-armed bandits jumps to 200!

Yes, the older ships did have a glamour, a style, a nostalgic mystique about them, but the contemporary fleet is more purposeful, certainly splashier and unquestionably offering more in creature comforts. They are moving hotels: televisions in every room, hair dryers and computerized wake-up service, walk-in closets and individually set temperature controls. There are hot tubs on deck and open-air restaurants, specialty boutiques and even juice bars. And what about the growing fleet of luxury cruise yachts, the ships that carry 200 or less? Their all-suite configurations include private bars and stereo systems and even individual safes.

At the time of writing, in the summer of 1990, the cruise industry—particularly in North America—is booming, with close to $5 billion in annual sales. Over 150 ships are in international service and some three dozen more are either building or on the drawing boards. There seems to be no end. Perhaps substantial growth is still ahead. The 3.5 million passengers who took cruises from ports in the United States in 1989 represent only about 5 percent of all vacationers who can afford such voyages. They have to be recruited, to be "won over." A huge educational process, most of it through a blitz of television advertising, is under way.

This book is a photographic study of some of the great cast members of the pageant of the cruise-ship story. It goes beyond North American shores. Many readers will have memories of the earlier fleets: the *Santa Paula* to the Caribbean, the *Lurline* to Hawaii, the *Constitution* to the Mediterranean. But we soon see the transition, the changeover of the early seventies, to a new generation of ships, most of them Scandinavian-owned and everything about them aimed at the sea-going vacation. We also look at some of the smaller (and often secondhand) ships such as Italy's *Franca C.* and Turkey's *Ankara*, which are also part of the story. The eighties bring us to an era of "bigger and better." The legendary *France* is made over into the *Norway*, the likes of the exceptional *Royal Princess* and ultraluxurious *Europa* are commissioned and, in little more than a decade of doing business, Carnival Cruise Lines becomes the biggest fleet of all.

WILLIAM H. MILLER

The Sixties: Years of Transition

SAILING AWAY FROM old Pier 84 in New York, along that once-proud "Luxury Liner Row," when the city was still the biggest passenger-ship port on earth, seemed the start of one of life's great adventures. A sea voyage—a trip in a big ocean liner—a cruise! But cruising was not quite the common concept it seems to have become today. There had been a gala farewell: 2000 or so visitors to see off 600 passengers, bon-voyage parties in the public rooms and champagne (usually in paper cups) in the cabins, an old-fashioned band at sailing and masses of those colored streamers as the ship gently moved away from the dock. There was still an emotional exchange—that sense of parting. The sailing was one of the great rituals of an ocean-liner voyage. And it was an experience for the well-wishers too—to dress-up and party, to explore the ship, to feel something of the high-pitch excitement.

In late summer of 1967 the Greek *Queen Frederica* was one of the grandes dames of the Atlantic run of the period —40, historic and under her fifth house flag. She was also typical of the times. Many other cruise ships were older, former class-divided ships from the then-dwindling port-to-port trades. Often they had been readapted for leisure sailing—a pool or two placed on an upper deck, the air-conditioning system extended and private bathrooms

added to the lower-deck staterooms. The *Frederica* had been upgraded, but there were many telltale signs of a long career as well: lots of woodwork, clusters of often-painted overhead piping and wiring, and a musicians' gallery above the double-deck, period-style dining room.

Our five-day cruise to Bermuda cost $150, the absolute minimum rate. Twenty dollars a day was something of a bargain even then, and those B-deck quarters even included private showers. Such luxury! The food was good and plentiful (with an obvious Greek touch), the service crisp and the formal nights just that—formal. There was far more formal dressing, far more long gowns and dinner jackets, and a "Welcome Aboard" ball that included a greeting by the ship's master, a bemedaled admiral from the Royal Hellenic Navy. The sense of excitement seemed to persist to the very end, to that moment when we returned to Pier 84. Cruising was a special adventure then.

In this chapter, we look at the forerunners of the contemporary cruise business: Cunard's *Caronia*, one of the pacesetters and standard-makers, some of the big transatlantic superliners, the "honeymoon ship" *Queen of Bermuda*, the diverse careers of the sisters *Argentina* and *Brasil* and even some of the once popular European-based cruisers such as the *Andes* and *Reina del Mar*.

CARONIA—THE GREEN GODDESS.

Photographs of New York's Luxury Liner Row, the great steamship piers along the city's West Side, were often featured in newspapers and magazines. There the grandest transatlantic liners were to be found between their Atlantic crossings. The purpose of the passenger ship was to provide transportation from one point to another. On board, the accommodations varied from luxurious, upper-deck first class to more modest, less-expensive tourist class. By the 1960s, however, the airlines took their firm hold over the North Atlantic run (and eventually over all other ocean-liner routes) and so the number of such gatherings as this at New York dwindled. The big, older liners became dinosaurs—fewer and fewer passengers, mounting costs and increasing debts. Many went off to the scrapheap; others found new careers and profit in the cruise trades. Some made the transition easily and, with little alteration, became one-class, hotel-like ships that sailed "to the sun." The destination became less important and, in fact, more of a diversion.

This view from the early 1950s shows six noted Atlantic passenger liners: (from left to right) the *Constitution*, the *United States*, the *Liberté*, the *Queen Elizabeth*, the *Caronia* and the *Franconia*. The *Caronia* is specially noteworthy. She was the first major liner to be designed for full-time cruising. When her owners, the Cunard Line, commissioned her in 1948, they were taking an enormous gamble. Could a 34,000-tonner turn a profit on year-round cruises?

Cunard managers sensibly avoided the short, less-expensive cruise runs, concentrating instead on long, luxurious trips—around the world for three months, the Mediterranean for six and eight weeks, Scandinavia in the summer. The *Caronia* quickly developed a loyal following of passengers who came, year after year and voyage after voyage. It was all rather clublike. For about 15 years, the *Caronia* reigned as the finest cruise ship afloat—she set standards, lured the best clientele, featured the most diverse itineraries. Most important, she proved that big ships had a future in cruising. She was the forerunner to the contemporary fleet featured in these pages. [Built by John Brown & Company Limited, Clydebank, Scotland, 1948. 34,183 gross tons; 715 feet long; 91 feet wide. Steam turbines, twin screw. Service speed 22 knots. 932 passengers (581 first class, 351 cabin class); reduced to about 550 all-first class for longer cruises.]

The **Caronia**. The *Caronia*, a "very British steamer," had a cozy charm about her, with lots of woods, polished brass, oversize chairs and glossy lino floors. She was maintained to absolute perfection and was serviced by choice Cunard staff members. Within that company's long and illustrious fleet, she was the first to have a private bathroom in every cabin and the first to have a permanent outdoor swimming pool.

Her decor and overall style are reflected in these views of her Balmoral Restaurant *(above, top left)*, Observation Cocktail Bar *(above, top right)*, writing room *(above, bottom left)* and enclosed promenade deck *(above, bottom right)*.

The **Caronia.** The *Caronia*'s loyal but increasingly older clientele began to fall away by the mid-sixties. Some had defected to newer, flashier liners then joining the long-cruise trade. She had also become a very expensive ship to operate, a luxury item to Cunard accountants. The ship's problems were further complicated by Cunard's overall situation; facing a declining Atlantic fleet and consequent losses in general revenue. The *Caronia* was put on the disposal list.

When she was sold in 1968, it was rumored she would become a floating hotel on the Dalmatian coast. Instead, she endured the indignity of becoming a struggling Caribbean cruise ship, the *Caribia*.

She suffered a serious fire on her second trip and had to be towed back from the Caribbean to New York, where, caught in financial problems, she stayed around the port. Once, she was even given a parking ticket by the city's police department for illegal berthing. Although she was sold to Taiwanese shipbreakers in 1974, she never in fact reached her destination. She was wrecked at Guam during a ferocious storm while under tow, and broke in three. Later she was cut up on the spot.

In this view, taken toward the very end of her life, the *Caronia* is shown at Pier 56, at the foot of West 14 Street in Manhattan. The terminal was once a busy Cunard passenger berth.

STRUGGLING SUPERLINERS.

Attempts to press some of the most legendary transatlantic liners into cruise service were often thwarted by economics: They were too big and therefore too costly to operate with reduced capacities in specially converted one-class configurations. They were also ill-suited, lacking the vast lido decks and outdoor pools, the discos and casinos and the brightly colored lounges that suited tropical travel. Cunard, for example, had spent huge sums in an attempt to transform the original *Queen Elizabeth,* the largest ocean liner ever built, into a cruise ship. Among other touches, a big pool was installed and air-conditioning added throughout the ship. But even with $125 five-day trips from New York to Nassau and back, she failed. Retired in 1968 after a bid to make her a Florida hotel-museum (in the same way the *Queen Mary* had been converted in California), she was sold to a Taiwanese shipping tycoon, who planned to convert her into a combination cruiseship–floating university. She is shown above, renamed *Seawise University,* arriving at Hong Kong for her refitting in July 1971. At the end of this conversion, she burned, capsized and had to be scrapped. [Built by John Brown & Company Limited, Clydebank, Scotland, 1940. 82,998 gross tons; 1,031 feet long; 119 feet wide; 39-foot draft. Steam turbines, quadruple screw. Service speed 28.5 knots. 2,283 passengers (823 first class, 662 cabin class, 798 tourist class].

The *France (opposite, top),* the most famous Atlantic liner of her time—luxurious, faultlessly served, offering the best cuisine on any sea—was detoured off the traditional Atlantic and went cruising to the Caribbean, to Rio for Carnival and on two highly publicized trips around the world. On those lavish circumnavigations, at least one passenger took along his own chef, another had his favorite champagne flown in from his French vineyard and still another booked an extra suite just for her harp. But the great ship proved to be too expensive. Her French government subsidies were cut (going to the supersonic Concorde instead) and, in 1974, she went to lay-up at Le Havre. [Built by Chantiers de l'Atlantique, St. Nazaire, France, 1961. 66,348 gross tons; 1,035 feet long; 110 feet wide; 34-foot draft. Steam turbines, quadruple screw. Service speed 30 knots. 1,944 passengers (501 first class, 1,443 tourist class).]

A similar fate befell the *United States,* the fastest ocean liner ever built *(opposite, bottom).* Turning to cruising late in her career, she was troubled by high operating costs and frequent labor difficulties. She was laid up at Norfolk, Virginia in 1969. Despite numerous plans to revive her, including one for conversion to a novel condominium-style cruise ship, she has not sailed since. [Built by Newport News Shipbuilding and Dry Dock Company, Newport News, Virginia, 1952. 53,329 gross tons; 990 feet long; 101 feet wide; 28-foot draft. Steam turbines, quadruple screw. Service speed 32–33 knots. 1,928 passengers (871 first class, 508 cabin class, 549 tourist class).]

HONEYMOON QUEEN.

The two ships known as the "honeymoon ships" had convenient Saturday afternoon departures from New York to Bermuda. With prices starting at $150, the six-day round-trips ended on the following Friday morning. The *Queen of Bermuda* (shown opposite arriving at Hamilton, Bermuda) was the older and larger; the smaller *Ocean Monarch* was more yacht-like and was periodically sent off on longer trips to the Caribbean in winter and the St. Lawrence River in summer. Their British owners, the Furness-Bermuda Line, began to encounter increasingly stiff competition by the mid-sixties. The situation was further complicated by a new set of strict American safety regulations. In order to pass, the ships would need expensive overhauls. In 1966, Furness decided to end its Bermuda cruises. The *Queen* went, after 33 years of service, to ship breakers in Scotland and the *Ocean Monarch* to the Bulgarians, who renamed her the *Varna*. [*Queen of Bermuda*: Built by Vickers-Armstrongs Shipbuilders Limited, Barrow-in-Furness, England, 1933. 22,552 gross tons; 590 feet long; 77 feet wide. Steam turbo-electric, quadruple screw. 733 all-first-class passengers.]

INDEPENDENCE.

Some of the most popular cruises of the 1960s were the three-week Sunlane Cruises of the splendid American Export sister ships *Independence* and *Constitution*. Departing from New York, the ships sailed across the mild mid-Atlantic to Algeciras and then to Genoa and Naples. From that last Italian port, they reversed direction and traveled westward via Cannes, sometimes Barcelona, and then a return call to Algeciras before returning to New York. Minimum fares in 1960 were $715 in cabin class, $900 in first class. Round-trip passengers had the added excitement of traveling with one-way and port-to-port voyagers as well. With passengers changing almost constantly, the feeling was much like that of a large hotel. In this poetic view, the *Independence*, seen from a sailing boat as she is moored off Algeciras, is silhouetted by the late afternoon sunlight. [Built by Bethlehem Steel Company, Quincy, Massachusetts, 1951. 30,293 gross tons; 683 feet long; 89 feet wide; 30-foot draft. Steam turbines, twin screw. Service speed 23 knots. 1,110 passengers (405 first class, 375 cabin class and 330 tourist class).]

GO-GO CRUISES *(opposite, top)*.

By the sixties, American Export's transatlantic trade had begun to fade and so, like so many of their competitors, they sought alternatives. In 1968, the *Independence*, shown here, was reconditioned for full-time cruising, but in a mod, cruise-a-go-go color scheme (costing some $1 million and then said to be the most extensive paint job ever given to a passenger liner). Even a new marketing scheme was employed: $98 for a seven-day cruise, but with the cost of all food extra. It quickly failed to attract sufficient customers. Within a year, both the *Independence* and her former fleet mate, the *Constitution*, were laid up.

DUTCH DREAMBOAT *(opposite, bottom)*.

To the very end of her days, Holland-America Line's *Nieuw Amsterdam* was considered to be one of the most beautiful passenger ships ever to put to sea. Her perfectly proportioned exterior profile was matched by a splendid Art Deco European interior. Her main restaurant, for example, was one of her finest rooms and included a Morocco-leather ceiling and Murano-glass lighting fixtures. Used primarily on the North Atlantic run, she spent her winter off-seasons on the New York–Caribbean cruise circuit, usually on two-week trips to ports such as Nassau and Port-au-Prince, St. Thomas and Curaçao.

The *Nieuw Amsterdam* was also well known for her excellent service, good cooking and perfectionist maintenance. Holland-Amer-ica's was known as the "spotless fleet" and the *Nieuw Amsterdam* was for many years its flagship. Inevitably, she attracted a long and loyal following. One woman, who made 219 trips with Holland-America, did 60 of them on the *Nieuw Amsterdam*, her favorite ship. It was a sad occasion when, in 1973, after 35 years of successful service, this grande dame went off to a Far Eastern scrapyard. [Built by Rotterdam Drydock Company, Rotterdam, The Netherlands, 1938. 36,982 gross tons; 758 feet long; 88 feet wide; 31-foot draft. Steam turbines, twin screw. Service speed 21 knots. 1,157 passengers (574 first class, 583 tourist class).]

THE GROANING BOARD *(above)*.

Most of the great shipping companies took great pride in their kitchens. The menus were extensive (one fleet carrying six different kinds of breakfast bacon) and went to as many as eight different courses for dinner. The table settings were appropriately matched: fresh linen, hand-polished silver, gleaming crystal, fine china and a bouquet of flowers. In addition to the three main meals, there were also midmorning bouillon, afternoon tea and fabled midnight buffets. At those late-night culinary specials, such as this aboard the *Rotterdam*, there would be the likes of carved barons of beef, elaborate baked concoctions and, as centerpieces, intricately carved ice sculptures.

WHITE VIKINGS *(above, left)*.

The Swedish American Line had a prized, much-envied reputation for its cruising. Their ships, the *Kungsholm* and *Gripsholm* (the latter shown arriving at New York on her maiden voyage in May 1957), spent more than half their year on luxury sailings—around the world, around Africa and South America, the Mediterranean and Scandinavia, and the occasional shorter trip to the Caribbean and the Canadian Maritimes. Everything about them was praiseworthy and comfortable—they were like floating country clubs. Passengers returned year after year, often taking the same cabin and requesting the same dining-room table. Some women booked extra cabins for just their clothes; others brought along personal servants. One included her own chef among her retinue. Passenger lists included heiresses and industrialists, film stars and European royalty.

The Swedish American Line retained its large following but, by 1975, the high costs of national labor and fuel oil just about eliminated all profits. The ships had to be sold, the *Gripsholm* going to the Greeks to become the *Navarino* and later the *Regent Sea;* the *Kungsholm* later changing to Britain's P & O Company and being rechristened *Sea Princess*. [*Gripsholm:* built by Ansaldo Shipyards, Genoa, Italy, 1957. 23,215 gross tons; 631 feet long; 82 feet wide; 27-foot draft. Götaverken diesels, twin screw. Service speed 19 knots. 450 cruise passengers (maximum 778 berths).]

PROUD ITALIANS *(above, right)*.

The Italian Line was one of the best known of the transatlantic liner companies. Their latter-day fleet included four exceptionally modern liners: the sister ships *Michelangelo* (shown here) and *Raffaello*, the *Leonardo da Vinci* and the slightly older *Cristoforo Colombo*. They too made cruises and offered many Mediterranean trips. The *Michelangelo* and *Raffaello* often made three-week "Go-Round" cruises, which included not only Genoa and Naples, but Cannes and Barcelona and, occasionally, Casablanca and Lisbon. The *Colombo's* trips were longer and extended into the Adriatic, while in winter the *da Vinci* made an annual long trip that included the Holy Land, the Aegean and the Black Sea. But increased operational costs and all-too-frequent seamen's strikes eventually spelled their demise. Both the *da Vinci* and the *Colombo* finished up at the scrappers, while the comparatively new *Michelangelo* and *Raffaello* went to the Middle East to become Iranian military barracks ships. [*Michelangelo:* built by Ansaldo Shipyards, Genoa, Italy, 1965. 45,911 gross tons; 902 feet long; 102 feet wide; 34-foot draft. Steam turbines, twin screw. Service speed 26.5 knots. 1,775 passengers (535 first class, 550 cabin class, 690 tourist class).]

MAJOR CONVERSION.

One of the great forerunners of year-round Caribbean cruising out of New York was the Incres Line's *Victoria*. Commissioned while most liners still plied the class-divided route to Europe, she was a gamble at first, but soon had an admirable reputation, highlighted by her Italian service and cuisine (although the ship flew the Liberian flag of convenience). Internally, she was done in very contemporary styles (Mediterranean themes prevailed) and seemed the ideal size.

The *Victoria* also represented one of the most elaborate conver-

sions. She had been rebuilt in Holland in 1958–59, when just about every part of her was changed (including her engines and bow). Previously, she was the *Dunnottar Castle*, a class-divided, colonial passenger ship that was based at London for an extensive service around Africa. But when she first arrived at New York, in January 1960 (shown here), there was little left to hint of that earlier career. [Built by Harland & Wolff Limited, Belfast, Northern Ireland, 1936. 14,917 gross tons; 573 feet long; 71 feet wide; 28-foot draft. Fiat diesels, twin screw. Service speed 18 knots. Maximum 600 cruise passengers.]

CHANGING NAMES.

New York–based Moore McCormack Lines could not have imagined in the late fifties, when they commissioned their two finest liners, the *Argentina* and *Brasil (opposite, top)*, that they would undergo so many name changes. Initially used on the deluxe cruise run to the east coast of South America and later on more diverse cruising, they were sold to the Holland-America Line in 1972 and became the *Veendam* and *Volendam* respectively (shown above arriving at New York a year later). In 1975, to confuse things a bit, the *Veendam* went on a short charter and temporarily became the *Brasil*.

In 1976, they were both chartered to the short-lived Monarch Cruise Lines and they became *Monarch Star* and *Monarch Sun* respectively. They later reverted to their Dutch names and to further Holland-America service. Sold again in 1983–84, the *Veendam* became the *Bermuda Star* and then the *Enchanted Isle;* the *Volendam* changed to *Island Sun, Liberté, Canada Star (opposite bottom, with Bermuda Star), Queen of Bermuda* and finally *Enchanted Seas.* [Built by Ingalls Shipbuilding Corporation, Pascagoula, Mississippi, 1958. 23,500 gross tons; 617 feet long; 86 feet wide. Steam turbines, twin screw. Service speed 23 knots. 553 first-class passengers (now increased to approximately 720 each).]

SANTA ROSA (*above*).

The Grace Line's *Santa Rosa* and her twin sister ship, the *Santa Paula*, represented an earlier approach to cruise-ship design and operation. They were combination passenger and cargo ships, big "combo" liners with 300 first-class passengers and four holds of freight. They regularly ran 13-day cruises, leaving New York every Friday afternoon, with a prescribed Caribbean itinerary: Curaçao, La Guaira (for Caracas), Kingston, Nassau and Port Everglades. In 1960, minimum cabin fares started at $595.

Eventually the cruise-freight operations of these Santa ships ceased to be profitable, and in 1971 the pair was laid up. The *Santa Rosa* endured long neglect in Baltimore harbor; the *Santa Paula* was rebuilt as a stationary hotel ship. She was towed out to Kuwait where she served as the Ramada-Al-Salaam Hotel until damaged in the Persian Gulf War. [*Santa Rosa*: built by Newport News Shipbuilding and Dry Dock Company, Newport News, Virginia, 1958. 15,371 gross tons; 584 feet long; 84 feet wide. Steam turbines, twin screw. Service speed 20 knots. 300 first-class passengers.]

ABOARD THE SANTAS (*opposite*).

The center of nighttime activities on both Santas were the Club Tropicanas (*opposite, top*), with windows that looked out over the sea.

The enclosed promenade decks (*opposite, bottom*), a nice feature aboard the Santa liners, gradually disappeared from general cruise-ship design.

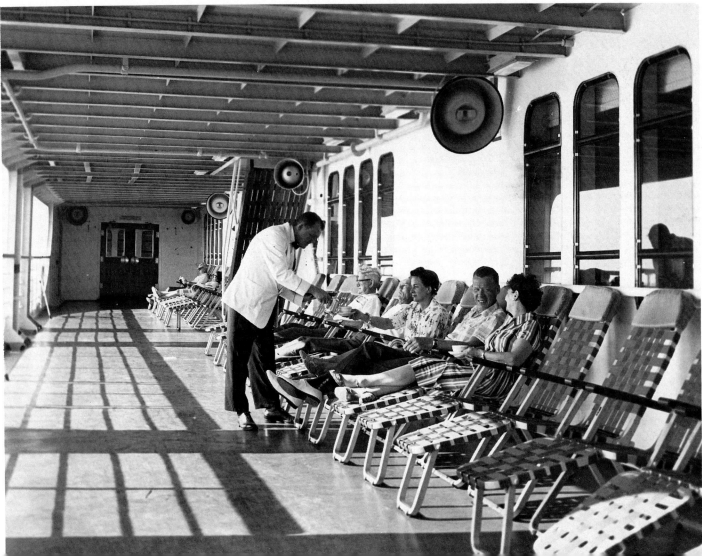

ROVING PRESIDENTS.

American President Lines ran a steady transpacific service: 43-day round-trips out of San Francisco and Los Angeles to Honolulu, Yokohama, Manila, Hong Kong, Kobe, Yokohama, Honolulu and then return to California, that were sold as both one-way passages as well as full cruises. In the sixties, their primary liners were the two-class sister ships *President Cleveland* and *President Wilson* and the all-first-class *President Roosevelt*. Their services prospered until late in that decade, by which time company managers had to experiment with more imaginative all-cruise itineraries. The President liners began to roam, from three-day long-weekend cruises down to Mexico's Ensenada, to two weeks northwards to Alaska (during which the *President Cleveland* is shown above, passing under Vancouver's Lion's Gate Bridge) and to a 65-day Mediterranean–Black Sea cruise and several three-month trips around the world. Inevitably, however, the high costs of running United States–flag passenger ships ended these cruises. The *President Wilson* was the last of the American President passenger liners by the time she was decommissioned in the spring of 1973.

The accommodations aboard the *President Cleveland* and her sister were typical of an American passenger ship: very modern, lots of stainless steel and all spit and polish. Many travelers preferred them because of their high standards of safety and cleanliness. Americans selected them because of their friendly service and good cuisine. The ships' interiors (as demonstrated by a view of the main lounge on the *President Wilson* shown opposite, top), maintained to the very end of their careers, reflected their late 1940s construction. [*President Cleveland*: built by Bethlehem Steel Shipyard, Inc., Alameda, California, 1947. 18,962 gross tons; 609 feet long; 75 feet wide; 30-foot draft. Steam turbo-electric engines, twin screw. Service speed 20 knots. 511 all-first-class passengers in 1972.]

THE HAWAIIAN RUN (*opposite, bottom*).

Among the most popular from the West Coast were the Hawaiian sailings of the big Matson liners *Lurline* of 1932 (seen here) and *Matsonia*. A five-day sailing from San Francisco or Los Angeles, it remained popular even as aircraft expanded their services. In later years, 15-day "Makahiki cruises" to Oahu, Kauai, Maui and Hawaii were so well patronized that the Matson Line formed its own Mariner Club for repeaters. Membership cards were issued and special incentives offered. By 1965, there were over 20,000 members and the club remains in existence. Matson also ran longer cruises: 42-day round-trips to the South Pacific Islands, New Zealand and Australia on the *Mariposa* and *Monterey*. These ships were somewhat smaller, having been converted from freighters, and had limited accommodations for 365 first-class passengers only.

The bigger Matsons went on in later years to cruising under Greek management. The original *Lurline* was sold in 1963 and became the Chandris Lines' *Ellinis*. She was finally scrapped in the late 1980s. The *Matsonia*, which had been the original *Monterey*, became the *Lurline* after her namesake was sold. In 1970, she joined Chandris and became the *Britanis*. The ship will have reached her sixtieth year of cruise service in 1992. [*Lurline*: built by Bethlehem Steel Company, Quincy, Massachusetts, 1932. 18,564 gross tons; 631 feet long; 79 feet wide; 28-foot draft. Steam turbines, twin screw. Service speed 22 knots. 760 first-class passengers.]

FLORIDA AND THE CARIBBEAN.

The Eastern Steamship Lines of Miami were the pioneers of Florida cruising. They started up in the fifties with two veteran steamers, the sister ships *Evangeline* and *Yarmouth*. Their home base was Miami, then far from being the huge cruise port it is today. The Dodge Island terminal had not even been thought of and there were no convenient air-sea packages available. But popularity and success followed. In 1959, the company added a former transatlantic ship, the *Arosa Star*, which was renamed the *Bahama Star*. She was the innovator of twice weekly three- and four-day cruises to Nassau and back. Fares for the three-day trips began at $59, the four-day at $69. Other ships soon followed in her wake and such that currently (in 1990), the three- and four-day market is the fastest-growing part of the entire United States cruise industry.

The *Bahama Star* was forced out of service in 1968 by strict American marine safety regulations: she was simply too old. She was supposed to become a motel ship moored on the California coast, but in April 1970 she was lashed by a ferocious hurricane at Oxnard and capsized (*above*). Her wreckage had to be scrapped on the spot. [Built by Bethlehem Steel Company, Quincy, Massachusetts, 1931. 7,114 gross tons; 466 feet long; 60 feet wide; 24-foot draft. Steam turbines, single screw. Service speed 15 knots. 735 first-class passengers.]

Eastern Steamship Lines also had the *Ariadne* (*opposite, top*), a yachtlike cruise ship for longer, more diverse Caribbean sailings. She was one of the first ships to sail to Cozumel off Mexico's east coast. Acquired from the Hamburg-America Line in 1961, she carried only 239 passengers who were looked after by a staff of 165. She had high-standard decor featuring mahogany paneling, fire-places and mosaics. Her swimming pool was placed forward rather than in the customary aft-deck position. Noted for her intimacy, the *Ariadne* became so popular as to have an enviable 30 percent repeat rate. She later passed to the Greek Chandris Lines and, with the elimination of a single letter, became the *Ariane*. [Built by Swan, Hunter & Wigham Richardson Limited, Newcastle-upon-Tyne, England, 1951. 6,644 gross tons; 454 feet long; 58 feet wide; 19-foot draft. Steam turbines, single screw. Service speed 18 knots. 239 first-class passengers.]

Another Florida "pioneer" cruise firm was the P & O Steamship Lines (standing for Peninsular & Occidental and not to be confused with Britain's far larger, better-known P & O Lines—the Peninsular & Oriental). This Miami company ran their single ship, the *Florida* (*opposite, bottom*), on regular cruises to Havana. When, in the late fifties, the political situation there changed, they shifted to twice-weekly trips to Nassau. She was later replaced by a chartered Israeli cruise ship, the *Jerusalem*, which sailed under the new name *Miami*.

The *Florida* had a long life. Retired in 1966, she was later sold to Canadian interests, who renamed her *Le Palais Flottant* (The Floating Palace) and sent her to Montreal for the Expo 67 celebrations. She served as a floating hotel for visitors. In June 1968, she was sold again, this time to Spanish ship breakers. Her last trip was a long tow across the mid-Atlantic to Valencia. [Built by Newport News Shipbuilding and Dry Dock Company, Newport News, Virginia, 1931. 4,956 gross tons; 388 feet long; 56 feet wide; 20-foot draft. Steam turbines, twin screw. Service speed 19 knots. Approximately 500 one-class passengers.]

BRITISH CRUISING.

Cruising from British ports had been very popular in the period before the Second World War, particularly in the otherwise hard-pressed thirties. It slowly revived in the 1950s, but reached its peak in the following decade. It has since declined considerably, especially in face of numerous air–sea holiday packages that join cruise liners in tropical ports, by eliminating the often difficult passage through the Bay of Biscay.

P & O, the historic shipping firm best known for its association with colonial India, the Far East and Australia and New Zealand, had the biggest passenger-ship fleet in the world in 1960: 16 liners in all. They all ran so-called "line voyages," but many of them also periodically detoured for cruising, from three-day minicruises to Amsterdam, two- and three-week "sunshine cruises" to the Mediterranean and then to three- and four-month trips around the world (P & O regularly called in at over 100 ports overseas). These cruises were often run on traditional two-class patterns: upper-deck first class; simpler, less-expensive tourist class. The differences were exemplified by professional entertainment in first class and passenger-created diversions in tourist.

The mighty *Canberra*, then P & O's premier ship, was certainly one of the most exceptional liners of her time, the biggest passenger ship ever to sail on the Australian route. She was also fast and well-appointed and had the largest overall capacity of any big liner of her day. Her designers used the then new engines-aft approach, which created more midships deck space and fewer intrusions into the center passenger spaces as well. Almost all later liners followed this pattern. Her only disadvantage was her draft: Through a miscalculation at the time of construction, she was too deep to allow her to put into many smaller cruise ports. She is seen above on an Australian trip, undocking from Sydney's Circular Quay, with the famed Harbor Bridge in the background. [Built by Harland & Wolff Limited, Belfast, Northern Ireland, 1961. 45,733 gross tons; 818 feet long; 102 feet wide; 32-foot draft. Steam turbo-electric engines, twin screw. Service speed 27.5 knots. 2,272 passengers (556 first class, 1,716 tourist class).]

P & O.

Because they were specially designed for the Australian service, almost all of the P & O–Orient liners (the fleet was actually a combination of two London-based shippers, P & O and the Orient Line) had more than ample top-deck space, the prime consideration being the steamy passages in the Red Sea and Indian Ocean in particular. Consequently, they were ideal for cruising—"Come to the sun with P & O," was one advertising slogan. The first-class pool aboard the *Oriana*, shown at left, was a very popular daytime spot.

The *Orcades* (above), one of the older P & O liners, is shown on a 15-day summer cruise out of Southampton in this view taken at Gibraltar. Her ports of call included Messina, Kotor, Corfu, Gibraltar and Lisbon. Three other British-based cruise ships are berthed in the background: Shaw Savill's *Ocean Monarch* to the left; Union Castle's *Reina del Mar* in the center (partially obscured); and the Chandris *Ellinis* on the right. A total of 4,800 passengers had been landed on Gibraltar for a day's touring and duty-free shopping.

NIGHTTIME SAILINGS *(opposite, bottom).*
There is nothing quite as evocative as a nighttime sailing. The ship is all aglow—the rows of lighted portholes, bright windows along the upper decks, the funnel bathed in floodlights and strands of yellow bulbs strung between the masts. Passengers board, receive a smiling welcome and enter the main foyer. A steward takes their hand luggage, directions are given to the cabins and, almost immediately, a warm, homelike sense begins to take hold. The ship becomes the home away from home. Passengers soon settle into their staterooms, cases are unpacked, personal items spread about. The mighty whistles sound and the ship itself rattles. Visitors have gone ashore, passengers line the outer decks and soon, with those final blasts, the deck crews undo the lines. The ship separates itself from shore. Tugs do the maneuvering and the liner is quickly in midstream. The lighted cityscape—New York or San Francisco or Sydney—is before you—much like a fantasy kingdom of lights. The ship is soon off, the vista of the harbor gradually fades.

In this scene, P & O's *Chusan,* using the Holland-America pier, is about to sail from New York, bound for a long cruise to South Africa.

ALASKA *(opposite, top).*
Beginning in the late fifties, because of its extensive round-the-world sailings, P & O became well known along the West Coast—at Los Angeles, San Francisco and Vancouver. Some cruise-only voyages were later added to the schedules. In the late sixties the *Arcadia* became one of the first big liners to cruise what were then unusual waters: Alaska's Inside Passage. She is shown here amid the majesty of Glacier Bay National Park. To such customary ports of call as Aden and Bombay, Melbourne and Sydney, she now added

Juneau, Skagway and Sitka. [Built by John Brown & Company Limited, Clydebank, Scotland, 1954. 29,734 gross tons; 721 feet long; 91 feet wide. Steam turbines, twin screw. Service speed 22 knots. 1,382 passengers (647 first class, 735 tourist class).]

THE EMPRESSES *(above).*
Canadian Pacific was another notable transatlantic shipping company, one especially known for its Empress liners, which plied the St. Lawrence River route between Liverpool and Montreal. But in the sixties they began to be hit by airline competition and turned to cruising. Two of their liners, the *Empress of Britain* (seen here sailing from Liverpool's Gladstone Dock) and her sister, the *Empress of England* (shown at berth), were even chartered out for an experimental venture. They joined the TSA (Travel Savings Association) in which cruise travelers invested their money in a savings plan and received inexpensive cruises as a form of interest. As examples: a two-week Mediterranean cruise cost £110 in first class, £35 in tourist; a month in the Caribbean went for £242 in first and £76 in tourist. An imaginative approach, especially to bring cruise travel to travelers who might not otherwise have gone, it later failed and the ships were eventually sold by Canadian Pacific. [*Empress of Britain:* built by Fairfield Shipbuilding & Engineering Company, Glasgow, Scotland, 1956. 25,516 gross tons; 640 feet long; 85 feet wide; 29-foot draft. Steam turbines, twin screw. Service speed 20 knots. 1,054 passengers (160 first class, 894 tourist class). *Empress of England:* built by Vickers-Armstrongs Shipbuilders Limited, Newcastle-upon-Tyne, England, 1957. 25,585 gross tons; 640 feet long; 85 feet wide; 29-foot draft. Steam turbines, twin screw. Service speed 20 knots. 1,058 passengers (160 first class, 898 tourist class).]

HOLIDAY SAILINGS *(above)*.

Through the 1960s and into the early 1970s, the week before Christmas still found the New York docks lined with Caribbean-bound liners, all of them filled to capacity, heading off on holiday trips that usually completed their returns just after New Year's. In this view of December 1968, nine liners can be seen (and almost the same number were at piers in other parts of the port). In mid-Hudson, the Swedish American *Gripsholm* has just departed, her empty slip soon to be occupied by the inbound *Empress of Canada*, the flagship of Canadian Pacific (retitled CP Ships). At berth, from left to right, are: the *Queen Anna Maria*, Greek Line; *Leonardo da Vinci*, Italian Line; *France*, French Line; *United States*, United States Lines; *Victoria* (mostly hidden), Incres Line; *Oceanic*, Home Lines; and *Homeric*, Home Lines (also partly hidden). By the late 1980s, however, the New York Christmas-cruise sailing list showed but a single departure. Passengers favored more convenient Florida- and Caribbean-based sailings.

MORE BRITISH CRUISE SHIPS *(left and opposite)*.

Perhaps the most novel, and certainly among the most popular forms of, British cruising was the British India Line's educational cruises. Its ships were specially converted (with dorms, lecture halls, etc.) for a passenger list of approximately one-quarter regular passengers and three-quarters students. A superb on-board lecture program was usually coordinated with the ports of call (the Mediterranean, Scandinavia, the Scottish Isles and the French château and wine districts). The regular passengers, who occupied the ship's original, high-standard quarters, attended these talks. These cruises often proved to be especially enriching travel experiences and consequently were often booked well in advance.

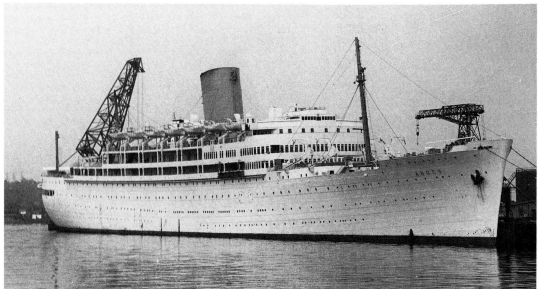

The most beloved of this fleet was the *Uganda (above, top)*, a former passenger-cargo ship on the old colonial run to East Africa. Here it is shown at Hamburg in 1967–68 undergoing conversion for schools' cruising. She carried hundreds of thousands of passengers and students alike over the years, and later proved a heroic ship when she was called for hospital-ship duties during the Falklands War.

In 1983, the *Uganda* ran the very last of the educational cruises. By then the vastly inflated economics of operating a cruise ship pushed fares to the point where they became unaffordable for many students and their families. [Built by Barclay Curle & Company Limited, Glasgow, Scotland, 1952. 16,907 gross tons; 540 feet long; 71 feet wide. Steam turbines, twin screw. Service speed 16 knots. 1,226 passengers (306 adults, 920 students).]

Royal Mail Lines' *Andes (above, bottom)*, once the British pride on the old South American run, was made into a cruise ship during an extended refit in 1959–60. She became the U.K.–based version of Cunard's *Caronia*: select and clublike, well served, offering magnificent food and diverse itineraries. The same passengers came year after year, often booking the same cabin and the same restaurant table at the same time of year. To many, she was like a large, white yacht. Her repeater following was called "Club *Andes*." On at least one sailing, all of her passengers were said to be titled.

But while her owners considered a replacement, age (with its mechanical and operational problems) set in. In February 1971, she ran her last cruise, a nostalgic six-week trip out of Southampton to Lisbon, Tenerife, Rio de Janeiro, Recife, Trinidad, Curaçao and Ma-

deira. That spring, she was sold to Belgian scrappers. Here she is shown at Ghent, her masts cut down, her two big tender launches already gone and her silent interiors awaiting the wrecking crews. [Built by Harland & Wolff Limited, Belfast, Northern Ireland, 1939. 26,860 gross tons; 669 feet long; 83 feet wide. Steam turbines, twin screw. Service speed 21 knots. 500 all-first-class passengers.]

Another extremely popular British cruise ship was the *Reina del Mar* of the Union Castle Line *(opposite, bottom)*. She too had first been used on the South American run, but for the Pacific Steam Navigation Company. She turned to full-time cruising in 1963, but while the *Andes* catered to aristocratic Britain, the *Reina del Mar* sought corporate Britain, the businessmen and their families. She tended to run two-week cruises, to the Canaries, West Africa, the Mediterranean and occasionally, in summer, to Scandinavia. In winter, when the British cruise trades lagged because of the bad climate, the ship shifted to South African service, sailing from Capetown to the Seychelles, Mauritius and even on gala trips across the South Atlantic for Carnival in Rio.

In 1973, when the cost of marine fuel oil soared from $35 to $95 a ton, ships such as the *Reina del Mar* could no longer break even. She was retired within a year and, with no foreign buyers interested, she went rather prematurely to Taiwanese scrappers, who finished her off in the winter of 1975–76, a period when many of her British-flag contemporaries were also ending their days. [Built by Harland & Wolff Limited, Belfast, Northern Ireland, 1956. 21,501 gross tons; 601 feet long; 78 feet wide. Steam turbines, twin screw. Service speed 18 knots. 1,026 cruise passengers.]

STELLA POLARIS.

One of the most classical ships in the international cruise trade was the Swedish-flag Clipper Line's *Stella Polaris*. She was built especially to resemble a large royal yacht, her design even including an ornate clipper bow. Actually, she was very much the commercial yacht, carrying 165 passengers who were looked after by an equal number of staff in cozy luxury and wood-paneled comfort. Needless to say, she had a very loyal following.

By the sixties, her annual pattern was established: winters in the Caribbean out of New Orleans, spring in the Mediterranean, sum-

mers in Scandinavia and an autumn return to the Mediterranean. It was difficult to replace her when she reached mandatory retirement age in 1969. While she might have been scrapped, she was preserved in distant waters. Bought by Japanese interests and renamed *Scandinavia*, she became a floating country club moored off Mitohama Beach. [Built by Götaverken Shipyard, Gothenburg, Sweden, 1927. 5,209 gross tons; 416 feet long; 51 feet wide. Burmeister & Wain diesels, twin screw. Service speed 15 knots. 165 first-class passengers.]

New Generation: The First Wave

On a day late in spring in 1973, I had a special treat: I joined the world's newest cruise ship for the last hour or so of her maiden voyage. We boarded from a tug in New York's Lower Bay. The splendid *Vistafjord*, representing the new age of cruise ships, had joined what many called the "Scandinavian armada." In the early seventies, there seemed to be a flood of new cruise-ship firms, many of them Oslo-based. The Norwegians, in particular, using their vast fortunes made with freighters and tankers, saw a bright future in cruising the Caribbean, services out of Miami offering a special lure.

Norwegian Caribbean Lines (now Norwegian Cruise Lines) was the pioneer. They had built a small ferry–cruise ship, the *Sunward*, for the England-to-Spain "sunshine" trade, but had problems from the start (most created by British currency restrictions imposed on overseas travel). The new ship needed an alternative service and her owners decided to gamble on Miami. It was a runaway success and soon successively larger and improved versions of the *Sunward* followed. Royal Caribbean Cruise Lines came next, introducing a trio of the more sophisticated ships of the day: raked bows, midships pools, a Broadway musical theme to their decoration and, perhaps most distinctive, a nightclub fitted atop funnels. They too proved an enormous success; others followed.

Royal Viking Line was the exception. They too built a trio of deluxe liners, but not for the Caribbean or short-distance trips. Carrying a capacity reduced to about 550 passengers (who were attended by a crew of about 400), these ships were the luxurious successors to the *Caronia*, the *Gripsholm* and the *Bergensfjord*, those yacht-like, "long-cruise" liners. Accordingly, the Royal Viking itineraries ranged from two or three weeks to as much as 100 days: the Mediterranean, Scandinavia, Alaska, around South America and annual circumnavigations of the globe. They quickly won a loyal following.

In the summer of 1972, when I visited the very industrious Wärtsilä Shipyards at Helsinki, I had come across two of these new-generation liners for the first time. The *Royal Viking Sea* and the *Sun Viking* were moored together at the fitting-out berth. Even incomplete and partially masked by scaffolding and painter's ladders and platforms, they looked incredibly futuristic. Unquestionably, they were part of the new breed.

Thus, less than a year later, the mood for the future of passenger shipping was bright and optimistic as the *Vistafjord* arrived in New York. Slowly, we sailed along the Upper Bay and then into the Hudson River. An escort of tugs and pleasure craft followed alongside, and fireboats spouted sprays of water. Helicopters buzzed overhead and then a booming band welcomed the ship as she was nudged by tugs into her berth. The excitement was electric.

"THE SHIP OF TOMORROW" (above).

When she arrived in New York for the first time, in April 1965, she was called "the ship of tomorrow." At over 39,000 tons, she was the largest liner yet built for full-time, year-round cruising. Owned by the Home Lines, which was a multinational ship-owner (Swiss-based, Italian-staffed and registered in Panama) of a type becoming typical, she was originally intended as a two-class transatlantic liner, trading between Northern Europe and the St. Lawrence. Only in winter would she cruise. But there had been some rethinking, especially in view of the rapidly declining Atlantic business, and she was placed instead on weekly New York–Nassau cruises from the very start. A $40-million ship, she was a huge success, copied and studied by her competitors and booked to capacity a full year in advance. Contemporary in every sense, her stunning decor incorporated Mediterranean themes; every cabin had private bathroom facilities and her twin pools were covered by a retractable glass Magrodome. In many ways, the *Oceanic* was the most important cruise ship of her time.

She is shown here about to sail from Berth 1 in November 1974, after the conclusion of the opening ceremonies of New York's Consolidated Passenger Ship Terminal. The Norwegian *Sea Venture* is in the opposite slip. [*Oceanic:* built by Cantieri Riuniti dell'Adriatico, Monfalcone, Italy, 1965. 39,241 gross tons; 782 feet long; 96 feet wide. Steam turbines geared to twin screw. Service speed 26 knots. 1,601 cruise passengers.]

SAGAFJORD (opposite).

In the mid-sixties Norwegian-America Line planned a new liner, to be called *Norway*. She was intended for divided service: two-class North Atlantic crossings between Oslo and New York for about six months, cruises for the other half of the year. Delivered as the *Sagafjord* in October 1965, cruising was her mainstay almost from the very start. She quickly established a sterling reputation, especially for longer, deluxe cruises. She was, like the earlier *Caronia*, like a big yacht, 450 or so passengers being looked after by an equal number of crew in a very spacious 24,000-ton ship. Even after being sold to Cunard in 1983 (but retaining her well-known name), she maintained her enviable reputation in the international cruise fleet. She was given an unparalleled 5 1/2 stars—the highest rating—by one cruise connoisseur and was voted "Ship of the Year" on several occasions by an organization of cruise-travel buffs. To date, she remains a ship that sets standards. The *Sagafjord* is shown here on a wintry day in the late sixties at New York's Pier 40, the big and innovative Holland-America Line terminal at the foot of West Houston Street. [Built by Société des Forges et Chantiers de la Méditerranée, Toulon, France, 1965. 24,002 gross tons; 615 feet long; 82 feet wide; 27-foot draft. Sulzer diesels, twin screw. Service speed 20 knots. 450 and sometimes 600 cruise passengers (maximum of 789 berths).]

HAMBURG.

Another luxurious entrant of the late sixties was German-Atlantic Line's *Hamburg*, seen above arriving at New York for the first time, in June 1969. Her sleek design was capped by a novel hourglass-shaped funnel. The *Hamburg* was also one of the earliest ships to follow a new design trend for cruise ships: placing the pool and main lido area midships *(left)* rather than aft. Although it was originally intended that the ship be a part-time Atlantic liner, trading between Hamburg, the Channel ports and New York, in fact she was scheduled for cruises exclusively from the beginning. She made many longer trips: the Mediterranean and Black Seas, Africa, around South America and, later, Pacific sailings from a California base. Unfortunately, the high cost of West German ship operations, compounded by the dramatic increases in fuel oil costs in 1973–74, spelled an early end to her German-Atlantic service. Late in 1973, she was sold to the Soviets and became their *Maxim Gorky*—not for Party-member cruises out of Odessa and Leningrad, but for a long-term charter to the giant Neckermann Company of Frankfurt. In ways, she remained the German ship, for most of her passengers continued to be Germans. Briefly, however, just prior to starting her Soviet service, she was chartered to a major film company as a floating prop, appearing as the fictional *Britannic* in the movie *Juggernaut*. [Built by Deutsche Werft Shipyard, Hamburg, West Germany, 1969. 24,962 gross tons; 642 feet long; 90 feet wide. Steam turbines, twin screw. Service speed 21 knots. 600 cruise passengers (790 maximum).]

QUEEN ELIZABETH 2.
Unquestionably, the most important single liner of the late sixties was Cunard's *Queen Elizabeth 2*, commissioned in the spring of 1969, after considerable and expensive delays. An $80-million ship, she was completed to replace both the *Queen Mary* and the *Queen Elizabeth*, spending half her year on the traditional Cunard route between Southampton, Cherbourg and New York, and the other half in cruising. The general trend was toward ships of 15,000 to 25,000 tons and so it was felt that there would never again be a passenger ship of such dimensions—that she would be the last of the superliners. [Built by Upper Clyde Shipbuilders Limited, Clydebank, Scotland, 1965–68. 65,863 gross tons; 963 feet long; 105 feet wide; 32-foot draft. Steam turbines, twin screw. Service speed 28.5 knots. 2,005 passengers (564 first class, 1,441 tourist class).]

The *QE2.*

Almost everything about the new *Queen*—the *QE2* as she was quickly dubbed—was different. Even her profile, with its single mast above the bridge area and the lone funnel, seemed quite distant from the conservative public image that Cunard had maintained with earlier ships such as the previous Queens and the *Caronia.* Certainly, the decor was different as well. Formicas, stainless steel and plastics had replaced the wood panels of the past. The Double-Deck Lounge, the ship's main ballroom *(opposite, top),* and the Tables of the World Restaurant *(opposite, bottom)* are shown as examples of the "new Cunard."

The new Queen was very popular almost from the very start. Her transatlantic crossings were run like cruises, with fewer of the class distinctions of the past and far more on-board entertainment. These Atlantic passages held special appeal for a nostalgic clientele who mourned the passing of the earlier transatlantic superliners. Her cruises had the added distinction of being aboard "the largest liner sailing to the tropics."

The *QE2* made her first three-month around-the-world cruise in 1975. Soon after, in response to demand, it was decided to extend the ship's luxury quarters. Two special duplex penthouses were added in December 1978, during the ship's winter overhaul at a Bayonne, New Jersey shipyard in New York harbor *(above).* For years thereafter, these were the most lavish as well as the most expensive accommodations at sea. In the mid-eighties, on a 95-day world cruise, for example, they were priced from $100,000 per person.

CUNARD PRINCESS.

Apart from the mighty *QE2*, however, Cunard felt, as did so many others in the cruise business of the early seventies, that smaller, more economical and more efficient ships were the way of the future. Consequently, in 1971–72, it added the 14,000-ton sister ships *Cunard Adventurer* and *Cunard Ambassador*. They proved to be too small, and were replaced in 1976–77 by a larger, more suitable pair, the 17,000-ton *Cunard Countess* and *Cunard Princess* (the latter seen left at Cozumel with the Bermuda Star Line's *Vera Cruz* in the background). These ships, with British officers and multinational crews, could be deployed almost anywhere: the Caribbean, trans–Panama Canal, the Mexican Riviera, Alaska and, starting in 1989, to European waters for Mediterranean, Black Sea and West African cruising. The top-deck pool area aboard the *Cunard Princess* (*below*) includes not only a full pool, but two whirlpool tubs and a children's wading pool. While they were not quite the big, lavish Cunarders of the past, they have been pleasing to the home-office accountants. [*Cunard Princess:* built by Burmeister & Wain Shipyards, Copenhagen, Denmark; completed by Industrie Navali Merchaniche Affine Shipyard, La Spezia, Italy, 1977. 17,495 gross tons; 536 feet long; 74 feet wide. Burmeister & Wain–type diesels, twin screw. Service speed 20.5 knots. 750 cruise passengers.]

THE NORWEGIANS.

One of the most important cruise ships of the sixties was the little Norwegian *Sunward (opposite, top),* the first modern, amenity-filled cruise ship in the Florida–Caribbean trade. She started sailing under the newly created banner of Norwegian Caribbean Lines (it was thought best to emphasize the reputation of Norwegian seamanship and service). It was a success from the start. The *Sunward* had been a pioneer and, almost immediately, Norwegian Caribbean looked to further expansion. [Built by A/S Bergens Shipyard, Bergen, Norway, 1966. 11,000 gross tons; 458 feet long; 68 feet wide. Burmeister & Wain–type diesels, twin screw. Service speed 21 knots. 558 cruise passengers.)

Norwegian Caribbean turned to the West Germans for two improved, enlarged versions of the original *Sunward:* the *Starward* of 1968 *(above)* and, a year later, the *Skyward.* They each worked seven-day itineraries, the most popular in the Caribbean. One sailed to Puerto Rico and the Virgin Islands, the other to Jamaica. They were well received as "fly 'n' sail" ships: Passengers were flown in from diverse parts of North America, delivered (usually to the ships at Miami the same day) and returned, rested, happy and tanned, a week later. It was a magic formula.

Norwegian Caribbean decided to expand further with the sister ships the *Southward* and the *Seaward* of 1971–72. The *Southward* was commissioned as planned, but the *Seaward* project, complicated by rising Italian-shipyard costs, was abandoned. Restyled, the ship was later sold to P & O, which had it completed as the *Spirit of London.* [*Starward:* built by A/G Weser Shipyards, Bremerhaven,

West Germany, 1968. 12,949 gross tons; 525 feet long; 75 feet wide. M.A.N.–type diesels, twin screw. Service speed 21 knots. 747 cruise passengers.]

The cruise boom of the early seventies created a "Scandinavian armada." Most Norwegian shipowners saw tremendous promise in the American cruise industry (even if most of them had never even owned a passenger vessel of any kind). Groups of partners, shipowners who had become rich in freighter and the ever-growing oil-tanker fleets, created new cruise subsidiaries.

Isak M. Skaugen and Anders Wilhelmsen formed Royal Caribbean Cruise Lines, headquartered at Oslo, but based at Miami, and built a trio of sister ships. Exceptional for their time, with their severely raked bows and interior decor taking themes from Broadway musicals, they were completed as the *Song of Norway* in November 1970; the *Nordic Prince* (shown opposite, bottom at Helsinki) in July 1971; and the *Sun Viking* in December 1972. As cruise ships became more and more specialized, especially for warm-weather voyaging, each of this trio was fitted with a cocktail bar built out of the aft funnel. Reached by a separate rear stairwell, this popular facility gave passengers a 180-degree view of the stern section and the sea below. It was often busiest in the hour or so before dinner, when passengers, sipping a margarita or nursing a martini, could watch one of those fiery Caribbean sunsets. [*Nordic Prince:* built by Wärtsilä Shipyards, Helsinki, Finland, 1971. 18,416 gross tons; 550 feet long; 80 feet wide; 22-foot draft. Sulzer diesels, twin screw. Service speed 21 knots. 876 cruise passengers.]

ROYAL VIKING LINE.

Royal Viking Line, a creation of three Norwegian shipowners (the Bergen Line and the Nordenfjeldske and Klaveness companies) was not intended for the one- and two-week Caribbean cruises that were continually growing in popularity. Royal Viking's intentions were aimed instead at deluxe cruising to ports all around the world. In fact, so lengthy and diverse were its schedules and itineraries that the company booklet in which they were published was aptly called "the atlas."

The company built three sisters—the *Royal Viking Star* (introduced in September 1972), the *Royal Viking Sky* and the *Royal Viking Sea*—as the contemporary versions of Cunard's long-cruise classic, the *Caronia*. The new trio was promptly acclaimed for their beautiful interiors and perfectionist on-board style and service. They soon began to gather a loyal following of passengers who came on voyage after voyage.

The Royal Viking itineraries have included almost every imaginable cruise area: Alaska, the Amazon, the Aegean, the Baltic, the Black Sea, the Chinese coast and the "lost isles" of the Indian Ocean and the South Seas. The *Royal Viking Sea* is shown (*opposite, top*) arriving at Boston, a port of call during a two-week trip from New York to New England, the Canadian Maritimes and the St. Lawrence River. The *Royal Viking Sky* arrives early morning in Hong Kong (*opposite, bottom*) as part of a cruise that will include China, the Philippines, Indonesia, Singapore and Thailand. An idea of the ships' facilities is offered by views of the *Royal Viking Sky*'s Buccaneer Club (*right, top*) and the *Royal Viking Star*'s Bergen Lounge (*right, middle*) and aft decks (*right, bottom*). [*Royal Viking Sea:* built by Wärtsilä Shipyards, Helsinki, Finland, 1973. 21,897 gross tons; 581 feet long; 83 feet wide. Wärtsilä-Sulzer diesels, twin screw. Service speed 21 knots. 758 cruise-passenger maximum.]

PRINCESS CRUISES AND *LOVE BOAT* *(above)*.
Princess Cruises was created in the mid-sixties for an experimental winter service out of Los Angeles down to the Mexican Riviera—to Puerto Vallarta, Mazatlán and Acapulco. It prospered, but initially had to rely on chartered tonnage: Canadian Pacific's *Princess Patricia* (hence the name Princess Cruises) and then two Italian liners, the *Italia* and the *Carla C.* (advertised as the *Princess Italia* and the *Princess Carla)*. In 1974 the company was sold by its American owners to the P & O Group of Britain. Three ships were added immediately—the *Spirit of London,* which became the *Sun Princess,* and two Norwegian sister ships, the *Sea Venture* and the *Island Venture,* which became the *Pacific Princess* and the *Island Princess* respectively. From the start, their reputations were impressive. Also, in a stroke of marketing genius, Princess permitted the television series *Love Boat* to use the *Sun Princess* and then the *Pacific Princess* as a setting. The resulting publicity was incalculable; the effect on the entire cruise industry, enormous. The series, which reached tens of millions of Americans, promoted a very positive image for cruising: It was fun and available to everyone, not just older and richer vacationers. Within five years, *Love Boat* was cited as one of the three prime factors that influenced the growth of the cruise industry. It had prompted many travelers to take their first cruise (which almost always led to subsequent, often longer, voyages). The two other reasons were the convenience of air-sea package arrangements and the diversity of on-board amusements and entertainments, from aerobics and wine tastings to specialty-theme cruises arranged around such topics as jazz, Hollywood nostalgia and professional football. [*Pacific Princess*: built by Nordseewerke Shipyard, Rheinstahl, West Germany, 1971. 19,904 gross tons; 550 feet long; 80 feet wide. Fiat diesels, twin screw. Service speed 20 knots. 750 cruise passengers.]

HOLLAND AMERICA CRUISES *(opposite)*.
Holland-America Line became Holland America Cruises in its centennial year, 1973. The corporate headquarters were moved from Rotterdam to Stamford, Connecticut (later to Seattle) and its ships changed registry to the less costly, less-regulating Netherlands Antilles (Dutch West Indies). The homeport for the national flagship *Rotterdam (opposite, top)* and other company liners was now Willemstad on Curaçao. The last Dutch transatlantic crossing, run in September 1971, heralded a schedule entirely of cruises: the *Rotterdam* to Bermuda and Nassau, the sister ships *Veendam* and *Volendam* to the Caribbean and South America, and the *Statendam,* on longer, more expensive trips to the Mediterranean and Northern Europe.

Noted for her splendid decor, the *Rotterdam* features such accommodations as this deluxe double cabin *(opposite, bottom)* which, by 1990, was priced at $275 per person per day. [Built by Rotterdam Dry Dock Company, Rotterdam, The Netherlands, 1959. 38,645 gross tons; 748 feet long; 94 feet wide; 29-foot draft. Steam turbines, twin screw. Service speed 20.5 knots. 1,456 passengers (401 first class, 1,055 tourist class); 1,109 cruise passengers.]

CHANGES IN NEW YORK (opposite, top).

The growth of the North American cruise industry dealt a harsh blow to New York, once the ocean-liner capital of the world. The once-busy transatlantic companies virtually disappeared in the face of airline competition and some of the remaining cruise companies defected to such warm-weather homeports as Miami and Port Everglades.

In 1973–74, all but three of New York's Hudson River liner piers were closed. Even the comparatively new, innovative Pier 40 did not survive. The three that remained, former Piers 88, 90 and 92, stretching from West 48 to West 52 Streets, were rebuilt, refaced and made far more comfortable, with summer air-conditioning and winter heating. They were reopened in November 1974, but primarily for a seasonal business lasting from April through October. In this view, showing a busy Saturday morning in June 1975, six cruise ships are in port: Holland America's *Statendam* and *Rotterdam* are at original Pier 88 (now Berths 1 and 2); Home Lines' *Oceanic* and the Italian Line's *Michelangelo* at Pier 90 (Berths 3 and 4); Home Lines' *Doric* and Norwegian America's *Sagafjord* at Pier 92 (Berths 5 and 6). All of them were scheduled for cruises.

Long one of Holland America's most popular liners, the *Statendam* was sold in 1981 to the French-owned Paquet Cruises, becoming their *Rhapsody*. Still later, she went to the Greek-owned Regency Cruises as their *Regent Star*. [Built by Wilton-Fijenoord Shipyard, Schiedam, The Netherlands, 1957. 24,294 gross tons; 642 feet long; 81 feet wide. Steam turbines, twin screw. Service speed 19 knots. 952 cruise-passenger maximum.]

PRINSENDAM (opposite, bottom; above and below).

Holland America's first ship built specifically as a cruise ship was the *Prinsendam* of 1973 (opposite, bottom)—more intimate, designed for travels to smaller, more remote ports. At first routed on a year-round schedule of 14-day cruises out of Singapore to Indonesia, she later spent her summers in Alaskan waters.

Intended to be the first of a series of ships (the others never left the drawing board), the *Prinsendam* was another example of the prevailing trend among cruise-ship owners in the seventies toward smaller and more practical ships. Others were designed to take one full load of jumbo-jet passengers.

Among the ship's public areas, the night club (above, left) was located on the promenade deck and overlooked the bow area. The larger main lounge (above, right), with seating for 200, was a space convertible from entertainment center to late-night club.

Unfortunately, the *Prinsendam*'s career was cut short in October 1980 (opposite, bottom). While on a "positioning cruise," from Vancouver to the Orient, she caught fire off the Alaskan coast and had to be abandoned by her 524 passengers and crew. Despite salvage attempts, she sank some 50 miles west of Sitka. [Built by De Merwede Shipyard, Hardinxveld, The Netherlands, 1973. 8,566 gross tons; 427 feet long; 62 feet wide. Werkspor diesels, twin screw. Service speed 21 knots. 374 cruise passengers.]

SITMAR CRUISES.

For two decades the Monte Carlo–based Sitmar Line used austere, secondhand passenger tonnage, in the Europe–Australia emigrant and low-fare-tourist trades. They were hoping to expand and improve this when, in the late sixties, the Australian government's essential passenger contract was awarded to a rival, the Greek-based Chandris Lines. Consequently, Sitmar's two newly acquired ships, the former transatlantic Cunarders *Carinthia* and *Sylvania* needed reassignment. They were sent to Italian shipyards and

transformed into the cruise ships *Fairsea* and *Fairwind* respectively.

Sitmar created Sitmar Cruises and entered North American service in 1971. Unknown at first, it lost millions before establishing a strong reputation and following, based primarily on its Italian cuisine and service. The ships boasted triple swimming pools, the novelty of pizzerias and what was appraised as the best children's and teenage programs afloat.

The *Fairsea* was based on the American West Coast, sailing from San Francisco in the summers on two-week cruises to Alaska and

from Los Angeles for the remainder of the year, cruising to the Mexican Riviera (she is shown at Los Arcos, at Cabo San Lucas, the tip of Baja California). The *Fairwind* was the East Coast ship, based full-time at Port Everglades for 7–14-day Caribbean cruises. [*Fairsea*: built by John Brown & Company Limited, Clydebank, Scotland, 1956. 21,916 gross tons; 608 feet long; 80 feet wide. Steam turbines, twin screw. Service speed 19.5 knots. 910 cruise passengers.]

CARNIVAL CRUISE LINES (above).

One of the greatest success stories in contemporary cruising is that of Miami-based Carnival Cruise Lines, formed by Ted Arison, who had run the agency that once managed the rival Norwegian Caribbean Lines. He too saw tremendous promise in the Caribbean trade. Carnival began operations in February 1972, with the former *Empress of Canada* of Canadian Pacific, which had been renamed *Mardi Gras*, shown arriving at Miami for the first time. A former two-class transatlantic liner, her renovation for weekly cruise service was executed during her inaugural voyages. (At the time, Carnival did not have the additional capital for a shipyard refit.) Workmen traveled along with the first passengers, but were assigned to partitioned areas.

With a strong advertising campaign that emphasized the new company's informal, fun-in-the-sun mood and with lower and therefore more competitive pricing, Carnival scored a great success. It added its second ship in 1976, when the Greek Line's idle *Queen Anna Maria* became their *Carnivale*. In 1978, she was followed by the conversion of the big South African passenger mail boat *S. A. Vaal*, then one of the largest liners afloat, to the *Festivale*. Rebuilt in a Japanese shipyard (a novelty for passenger ships at the time), her subsequent tonnage of over 38,000 placed her among the largest cruise ships of the day. No sooner had the *Festivale* entered service, than the company ordered its first brand-new liner, the 30,000-ton *Tropicale*, which came from a Danish yard in 1980. [*Mardi Gras:* built by Vickers-Armstrongs Shipbuilders Limited, Newcastle-upon-Tyne, England, 1961. 27,250 gross tons; 650 feet long; 87 feet wide. Steam turbines, twin screw. Service speed 21 knots. 1,240 cruise-passenger maximum.]

DODGE ISLAND, MIAMI (opposite, top).

The Port of Miami, having expanded in the late sixties to the new Dodge Island complex seen here, witnessed spectacular growth, eventually becoming the biggest and busiest ocean-liner port in the world. In 1967, Miami handled 188,000 cruise passengers. There were 246,000 one year later and 610,000 by 1970. Thereafter, figures consistently showed impressive increases, reaching 3 million by 1989, with an anticipated 4 million by the year 2000.

In this early aerial view of Dodge Island, four cruise liners, all of them on three- and four-day trips across to the Bahamas, are seen in a Friday morning rendezvous. From left to right are the *Freeport II* of Bahama Cruise Lines, the *Flavia* of Costa Line and then the fleetmates *New Bahama Star* and *Emerald Seas* of Eastern Steamship Lines.

CARIBBEAN CRUISING (opposite, bottom).

The Caribbean remains the most popular cruise destination of all. It has been divided into four service areas: seven-day cruises to the Eastern Caribbean (Puerto Rico, the Virgin Islands and usually one other port); weekly trips to the Western Caribbean (Jamaica, Grand Cayman and the Mexican east coast ports of Cancún and Cozumel); weekly sailings to the Lower Caribbean from San Juan to ports such as Martinique, St. Maarten, Barbados, etc.; and, finally, the longer 10–14-day cruises that include Aruba and Curaçao, La Guaira (for Caracas and the prized distinction of stopping-off on continental South America), Cartagena (Colombia) and the Panama Canal.

In 1969, the most popular Caribbean cruise ports were the U.S. Virgin Islands (St. Thomas, St. Croix and St. John) with 166,117 visitors; San Juan was second, with 119,937; all the ports of Jamaica, 94,021; then Curaçao, Barbados, Martinique, the combined St. Maarten/Saba/St. Eustatius, Port-au-Prince, Grenada, Guadeloupe and Aruba.

This dramatic aerial view dates from February 1980, when a record number of 9,988 passengers went ashore at Charlotte Amalie on St. Thomas from 11 cruise ships. Along the dockside, from left to right, are the *Daphne* and *Carla C.* of Costa Line; *Sun Princess* of Princess Cruises; and *Cunard Countess* of the Cunard Line. At anchor, in the inner harbor, are the *Fairsea* of Sitmar, the *Doric* of Home Lines (just behind the *Fairsea*) and, smaller and to the right, the *Aquarius* of Hellenic Mediterranean Lines. In the far distance, above and beyond the *Doric*, is the *Amerikanis* of Chandris Lines.

More Distant Waters

OVER THE PAST 20 years, I have done a number of cruises that have originated in overseas ports. Gradually, the air–sea package has made this more and more convenient. There is often a restful hotel stay a night or so after arrival and before the sailing. By the mid-seventies passengers were becoming less and less reluctant to travel long distances. I have departed on cruises from London and Southampton, Amsterdam and Hamburg, Genoa and Venice and Athens' Piraeus. Even farther afield, I have joined cruise ships at Tokyo and Seoul, Honolulu and Hong Kong, Singapore and Sydney. The destinations have been as varied: the Baltic capitals and the Norwegian fjords, the Scottish isles and the Arctic icepack, the Costa del Sol and the Greek isles, the cities of China and backwaters of Indonesia.

The overseas cruise ship is different in tone from most of the other ships described in these pages. It is more international. Often, I have sailed with as many as a dozen different nationalities among the passengers and, inevitably, I once sailed as the only American passenger among 1,400.

Most ships included in this chapter represent these "different" voyages—the secondhand Mediterranean liners, the Greek ships with even longer histories and the Soviets with the largest passenger-ship fleet of all. There are also Communist trade-union cruises, riverboat cruises and Antarctic cruises. Certainly, these are among the most interesting if lesser-known cruise ships.

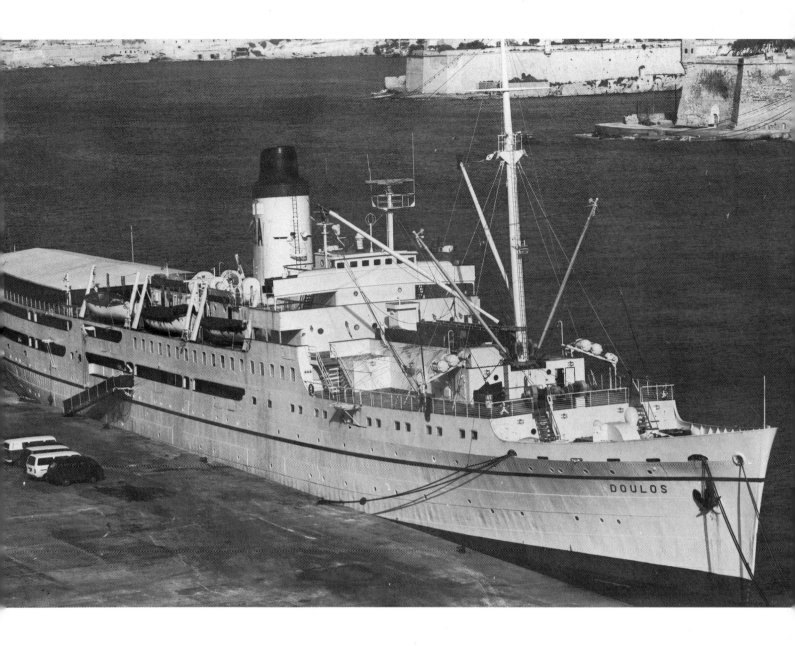

COSTA LINE.

Italy's Costa Line, which started its passenger services in the late forties on the European immigrant runs to Latin America, began periodic cruising a decade later. It developed such a strong following, based mostly on its Italian service and cooking, that, by the early 1980s, it owned the largest cruise fleet apart from the Soviets.

Costa's first real cruise ship was the little 6,500-ton *Franca C.*, a ship so greatly changed and modernized in so many ways that she belied her true age. Built in 1914 as the American freighter *Medina*, she was rebuilt in 1948 for passenger service (primarily immigrant). She was rebuilt again in 1959, this time for cruising and with very contemporary, clublike accommodations for 367 passengers only. She was re-engined as well, the original steam turbines being changed to Fiat diesels. Used in the summers for Mediterranean cruising out of Genoa, she sailed in the winters from Florida to the Bahamas and the Caribbean. She was one of the very first cruise ships to use Port Everglades regularly. In 1968, being shifted to San Juan, Puerto Rico, the *Franca C.* inaugurated the first air-sea combination cruises. These packages soon became popular for all cruises.

At the age of 63, in 1977, the *Franca C.* was retired from commercial service. But instead of going to the scrappers, she was sold to a missionary group that refitted her as the floating book fair *Doulos*. Roaming the globe (mostly to Third World lands) and with an all-volunteer crew, she remains in service at the time of writing (1990), aged 76 and certainly the oldest former cruise ship still about. [Built by Newport News Shipbuilding & Dry Dock Company, Newport News, Virginia, 1914. 6,822 gross tons; 428 feet long; 55 feet wide. Fiat diesel, single screw. Service speed 15 knots. 367 cruise passengers.]

E ITALIAN TRADE.

sta Cruises expanded to a worldwide operation by the early
80s. Its flagship, the *Eugenio Costa* (renamed from *Eugenio*
spent most of the year cruising from Genoa to the Eastern
editerranean. The smaller *Enrico Costa* cruised from Genoa as
ell, but to Western Mediterranean ports. The *Carla Costa*
uised full-time in the Caribbean, sailing out of San Juan. The
sters *Daphne* and *Danae* *(opposite, top;* rebuilt from freighters
the Greek-flag Carras Cruises in 1975–76, but then leased to
sta in 1979 and then finally bought outright five years later)
ided their schedules—the former between winters in the
ribbean and summers in Alaska (sailing from Vancouver),
e latter in Mediterranean waters out of Venice for most of the
ar and then departing each December on an annual four-
onth around-the-world trip. [*Danae:* built by Harland &
olff Limited, Belfast, Northern Ireland, 1955. 16,310 gross
ns; 533 feet long; 70 feet wide. Doxford diesels, twin screw.
rvice speed 17 knots. Approximately 500 cruise passengers.]

In the seventies, the Italian passenger fleet, although still
ite modern, began to face hard times. Used mostly in regular
er trades to such areas as the United States, South America
d Australia, they faced not only increasing competition from
e airlines, but escalating operational costs and all-too-fre-
ent strikes by worried crew members. Two of the biggest
ips, Lloyd Triestino's *Guglielmo Marconi* and *Galileo Galilei*
pposite, bottom),* were hard hit on their tourist and immigrant
ns from Genoa and Naples to Fremantle, Melbourne and
dney. Finally withdrawn, they were pressed into alternative
uise services, the *Marconi* out of New York to the Caribbean
d the *Galileo* in the Mediterranean (and later under charter to
eece's Chandris Cruises). But both ships needed upgrading
well as modernization to compete effectively and, in the
d, these attempts failed. They were laid up for a time, this
hotograph showing them nested together at a berth near
enoa Airport, in September 1983. Both ships were reacti-
ted, but as vastly different-looking ships: the *Marconi* as
osta Cruises' *Costa Riviera,* and the *Galileo* as the *Meridian* for
handris Celebrity Cruises. [Built by Cantieri Riuniti dell'Ad-
atico, Monfalcone, Italy, 1963. 27,907 gross tons; 702 feet long;
feet wide. Steam turbines, twin screw. Service speed 24
ots. 1,754-passenger maximum reduced to about 1,100 for
uising.]

Another well-known Italian liner on the long-distance Aus-
alian immigrant and tourist services was Lauro Line's *Achille*
uro (right).* After 1973, she too turned mostly to cruising—
 Mediterranean sailings, charter voyages out of South African
orts and even occasional around-the-world cruises. But it was
one of the Mediterranean trips that she achieved maritime
mortality. Making headline news almost everywhere, she
as seized, on October 7, 1985, by Arab terrorists and held for
vo days before being freed and returned to her owners. The
bject of two major films, at least one book and an opera, this
cident, which included the death of one American passenger,
d much to cause a temporary but devastating decline in
editerranean cruising. Several Greek cruise companies actu-
ly closed, many ships were laid up temporarily and some
her cruises were departing with as few as 100 passengers on
ard. [Built by De Schelde Shipyards, Flushing, The Nether-
nds, 1939–47. 23,629 gross tons; 631 feet long; 82 feet wide.
lzer diesels, twin screw. Service speed 22 knots. Approxi-
tely 1,652-passenger maximum reduced to about 980 cruise
sengers.]

IRPINIA *(above)*.

Italy's Siosa Lines developed a strong following for western Mediterranean cruises, with weekly sailings from Genoa to such ports as Cannes, Barcelona, Palma de Mallorca, Tunis, Capri and Naples. One of the favorites on this run was the *Irpinia*, a ship built in the late twenties for the French as the *Campana* and then bought by the Italians in 1955 for the Caribbean immigrant trade. She turned to full-time cruising in 1970, including periodic charter trips, such as London to the Norwegian fjords. (In this photograph, she is at anchor in the Geirangerfjord).

Earmarked for scrapping in 1976, she was given two reprieves. First, she was chartered to an American film company and then, fitted with twin dummy funnels, she portrayed the German liner *St. Louis* making its historic 1939 voyage to Havana with 900 Jewish refugees aboard in the film *Voyage of the Damned*. Afterward, her owners had second thoughts about retirement and restored her to Mediterranean cruising for several years. She was finally scrapped in 1983, aged 54. [Built by Swan, Hunter & Wigham Richardson Limited, Newcastle-upon-Tyne, England, 1929. 13,204 gross tons; 537 feet long; 67 feet wide. Fiat diesels, twin screw. Service speed 16 knots. 1,181-passenger maximum.]

OCEAN PRINCESS *(opposite, top)*.

In the sixties and seventies, there were also several new Italian cruise ventures as well. One, created by a consortium of national banks, was called Crociere d'Oltramare. Its first and only ship was the sleek-looking, engines-aft *Italia*. She represented the new generation of smaller, more intimate passenger ships. She was, however, put on charter work almost from the very start, sailing for the American-based Princess Cruises as their *Princess Italia*, although she was never formally renamed. In 1974, she was sold to the Costa Line and, as the *Italia*, began sailing on Mediterranean, Caribbean and South American itineraries. She was sold again, in 1983, to Ocean Cruise Lines and became their Bahamas-registered *Ocean Princess*. In winter, she sails the east coast of South America to coastal cities, along the Amazon and on occasional runs to Antarctica; in summer, she sails from Copenhagen to Norway and in the Baltic. She is shown here at the Danish capital along with three other cruise ships: the Soviet *Estonia*, East Germany's *Arkona* and the Norwegian *Sea Goddess I*. [Built by Cantieri Navali Feszegi Shipyards, Trieste, Italy, 1967. 12,219 gross tons; 490 feet long; 68 feet wide. Sulzer diesels, twin screw. Service speed 20 knots. 476 cruise passengers.]

MERMOZ *(opposite, bottom)*.

In the seventies, the French passenger-ship fleet declined considerably because of increasing operational costs and competition from less-expensive foreign-flag operators. One of the exceptions was Paquet Lines' *Mermoz*, a ship originally built in the fifties for the old West African colonial trades. She was converted for cruising in 1970. Since then, her itineraries have tended to be more unusual: remote ports along the Central American coast, the Galápagos, the Black Sea, the "lost isles" of the Indian Ocean and a highly reputed annual music festival at sea featuring top classical artists as onboard entertainers. Most recently, the *Mermoz'* clientele has been divided: about 75 percent European and 25 percent American. [Built by Chantiers de l'Atlantique, St. Nazaire, France, 1957. 13,804 gross tons; 530 feet long; 66 feet wide. Burmeister & Wain–type diesels, twin screw. Service speed 17 knots. 757 cruise-passenger maximum.]

VÖLKERFREUNDSCHAFT (above).

One of the most unusual cruise ships of the sixties was East Germany's *Völkerfreundschaft,* a name which translates as "Friendship among Nations." She became the world's first trade-union vacation cruise ship in 1960, carrying Communist Party members, workers and their respective families on subsidized "reward cruises" to the Baltic, the Black Sea, Egypt and occasionally as far afield as Havana. The political system she represented, however, often barred her entry to many other well-known cruise ports. On board, political lectures and work-related conferences often dominated the entertainment programs.

The *Völkerfreundschaft* had originally been a transatlantic passenger-cargo ship, Swedish American Line's *Stockholm,* and is probably best remembered for her collision, on July 25, 1956, with Italy's *Andrea Doria.* The latter sank while the smaller Swede returned to New York, most of her bow gone.

She was retired in 1985 and put up for sale. Rumors that she might become a museum and hotel ship in Stockholm harbor proved unreliable. She was used for a time as the Oslo-based *Fridtjof Nansen* to accommodate refugees from East and Southeast Asia. In 1989, she was sold once again, this time to the Italians, Starlauro Cruises, who planned (despite her advanced age and general condition) to rebuild her for Mediterranean and Caribbean cruising as the *Positano.* This scheme never materialized, and instead Lauro chartered a smaller Greek cruise ship (which became the *Angelina Lauro*) and then bought the former American liner *Monterey* (last used in the Hawaiian interisland trades). [Built by Götaverken Shipyards, Gothenburg, Sweden, 1948. 12,068 gross tons; 525 feet long; 69 feet wide. Götaverken diesels, twin screw. Service speed 19 knots. 568 one-class passengers.]

BLACK PRINCE (opposite).

In the mid-sixties, two well-known Norwegian shippers, the Fred Olsen Line and the Bergen Line, decided to replace some of their existing tonnage, but in a novel way. To economize, especially as shipbuilding costs were increasing, the new twin sister ships *Black Prince* and *Black Watch* shared operations. Fred Olsen would operate the ships in the off season for cruising (September through May), on two-week round-trips from London and/or Rotterdam to Madeira; Las Palmas, Teneriffe and Lanzarote in the Canaries; and occasionally to Lisbon, Cadiz or Agadir (Morocco). In the peak summer months, the ships, more like ferries, would ply the North Sea routes of the Bergen Line, sailing from Newcastle-upon-Tyne, England across to Bergen and Kristiansand in Norway, with periodic detours from Amsterdam and Cuxhaven (Hamburg) as well. For these voyages, the ships were renamed *Venus* and *Jupiter* respectively. Then, in autumn, they would revert to Fred Olsen and their "other" names.

Very popular, the *Black Prince* was specially converted for full-time cruising in 1986. She now sails to the Mediterranean and Scandinavia as well as the Canaries route (she is seen opposite, top, at Malta in 1987). Among her amenities is an aft marine platform for swimming, sunning and sailing that can be specially lowered when the ship is anchored offshore *(opposite, bottom).* [Built by Lübecker-Flenderwerke Shipyard, Lübeck, West Germany, 1966. 9,499 gross tons; 465 feet long; 67 feet wide. Pielstick diesels, twin screw. Cruising speed 18 knots, maximum speed 23 knots. 487 cruise passengers.]

SUN LINE.

Sun Line was the first to run luxury Greek island cruises. It began in the late fifties with a 1,900-ton converted Canadian warship, the *Stella Maris*. There was tremendous popularity in her twice-weekly, three- and four-day voyages to such romantic-sounding ports as Delos, Mykonos and Santorini. Several other ships were added, all of them in the smaller, yacht-like class. Still later, while financially linked to the mighty Holland-America Line and the Marriott Hotel Group, Sun Line decided to expand and increase to bigger ships, desiring to include winter and off-season services in the rapidly expanding, very lucrative U.S.–Caribbean market.

The French combination passenger-cargo liner *Cambodge* had just been put out of work by decolonization, the success of the airlines and the shift to containerization. Sun Line bought her, stripped her down to the hull and then had her rebuilt as the *Stella Solaris*. She was delivered in the spring of 1973 and, in many ways, appeared to be a brand-new ship. Her mainstay, the eastern Mediterranean itineraries, have included not only the idyllic Greek isles (where she is seen here) but calls at Istanbul, Haifa, Ashdod, Alexandria, Port Said and occasional calls at more remote Black Sea ports as well. From November through April, she detours to Caribbean and South American waters, including Amazon River trips, voyages through the Straits of Magellan and Panama Canal transits. [Built by Ateliers et Chantiers de France, Dunkirk, France, 1953. 10,595 gross tons; 532 feet long; 72 feet wide. Steam turbines, twin screw. Service speed 21 knots. 720 cruise-passenger maximum.]

STELLA OCEANIS.

Another Sun Line cruise ship, the *Stella Oceanis*, was at first well known for her extensive winter Caribbean cruises—14–21-day trips, sailing from San Juan and taking in some of the more remote ports of call, such as Anguilla, Bequia and Saba. In more recent years, she has remained in the Eastern Mediterranean (being laid up in winter). Her three- and four-day cruises are offered from April to October. The three-day weekend trips sail from Piraeus on Friday mornings and call at Mykonos (on the same afternoon), Rhodes, Kuşadasi (Turkey) and Patmos before returning; the four-day Monday departures go to Hydra, Heraklion (Crete), Santorini (where she is shown here) Rhodes, Kuşadasi and Mykonos. These cruises are particularly popular with European tour groups, who want to combine their visits to major cities with a short sea voyage and a glimpse of the fabled Aegean isles. [Built by Cantieri Riuniti dell'Adriatico, Monfalcone, Italy, 1965. 5,051 gross tons; 318 feet long; 52 feet wide. Sulzer diesels, twin screw. Service speed 17 knots. 367 cruise passengers.]

ROYAL CRUISE LINES (opposite, top).
The Royal Cruise Lines was formed in the early seventies with a special eye toward the expanding U.S. air–sea market. Company managers felt confident that American travelers were not only willing to endure flights to meet ships in Caribbean and Mexican ports, but to make even longer journeys to rendezvous with sailings in the Canary Islands, Italy and Greece. They built Greece's first brand-new cruise ship (all previous ships having been conversions), the 6,700-ton *Golden Odyssey*, which was designed to accommodate approximately one jumbo-jet load of passengers. It is seen here at the Panama Canal's Miraflores Lock. The initial foresight proved accurate and the company's fleet later expanded to include the 25,320-ton *Royal Odyssey* (the former *Doric* of the Home Lines) and then, in 1988, the new 40,000-ton *Crown Odyssey*.

In 1989, in an age of increasing cruise-ship mergers, Royal Cruise Lines was bought out by Norway's Kloster Group, the owners of the Norwegian Cruise and Royal Viking fleets. Initially, the only change seems to have been the transfer from Greek to Bahamas registry for the Royal Cruise vessels. [*Golden Odyssey*: built by Elsinore Shipbuilding & Engineering Company, Elsinore, Denmark, 1974. 6,757 gross tons; 427 feet long; 65 feet wide. Diesels, twin screw. Service speed 22.5 knots. 509 cruise-passenger maximum.]

EPIROTIKI LINES (opposite, bottom).
Epirotiki Lines, another Greek firm, is one of the giants of Mediterranean cruising. In fact, in 1955, it ran the first Aegean cruises out of Piraeus and then used the 1,900-ton *Semiramis*. Since then, the company, with over a dozen cruise ships within its fleet at times, offers itineraries in the Aegean as well as the Western Mediterranean, the Black and Red Seas, West Africa, Scandinavia and the Caribbean and South America. Epirotiki ships are also chartered on occasion on trips to such areas as the Canadian Maritime Provinces, South Africa and the Indian Ocean.

The company has, however, been made up entirely of second-hand tonnage, usually older ships rebuilt and given high-standard, contemporary decor. The *Apollo II* [Apollon], for example, shown here, was the former *Irish Coast* of Britain's Coast Lines. The company flagship for some time, the 15,000-ton *Atlas*, had been Holland-America's transatlantic liner *Ryndam* and the 12,000-ton *World Renaissance* was formerly Paquet's *Renaissance*. Other ships in the fleet include former deep-sea ferries, a Norwegian cruise ship and, perhaps most noteworthy, the former millionaire-class yacht *Argonaut*, which was built by Krupp of Germany in the late twenties.

[*Apollo II*: built by Harland & Wolff Limited, Belfast, Northern Ireland, 1952. 3,824 gross tons; 353 feet long; 51 feet wide. Burmeister & Wain–type diesels, twin screw. Service speed 17 knots. 350 cruise passengers.]

TYPALDOS LINES (above).
Another busy and energetic Greek shipper was the Typaldos Lines, which, by the mid-sixties, had amassed the biggest passenger fleet in the Eastern Mediterranean. It too preferred secondhand tonnage —older, usually, solid and strong ships capable of being rebuilt to suit special requirements. Its prize ships were two American-built sisters, Grace Line's *Santa Paula* and *Santa Rosa* of 1932, which, in 1961, became the *Akropolis* (shown here) and *Athinai* respectively. They ran the company's more diverse trips, often with German tourists on board, to the Black Sea, along the Adriatic, West Africa and sometimes to Scandinavia. The *Akropolis* was made over as more of a one-class cruise ship, whereas the *Athinai* became a three-class ship: 240 in first class, 180 in cabin class and 200 in tourist class. The latter also ran a two-week "express service" (which could be taken as a full cruise) from Venice to Split, Piraeus, Limassol, Haifa, Larnaca, Rhodes, Piraeus and then back to Venice.

Other Typaldos ships included the *Atlantica*, the former French-Caribbean liner *Colombie*; two more French vessels from the old Algerian trades, renamed *Mount Olympos* and *Poseidon*; and even two converted wartime seaplane tenders, the *Mykonos* and *Rodos*. But the entire Typaldos fleet collapsed, all because of a former British passenger-cargo ship, the *Leicestershire*, which had become the ferry *Iraklion*. On December 8, 1966, she sank in an Aegean storm with 241 casualties. In the investigation that followed, the ship was found to have been unsafely loaded. Typaldos was at fault and, in a test case, the owners were sent to jail. The fleet was quickly disbanded, the ships going to the scrap yards or to backwater anchorages (most in Pérama Bay near Piraeus) from which they would never again sail commercially. In 1978–79, the long-neglected, badly rusted *Athinai* had a reprieve: she was renamed *Titanic* for use in the film *Raise the Titanic*. In 1989, when she went to the breakers at nearby Aliağa in Turkey, she was probably the last survivor of that once mighty Typaldos fleet. [*Akropolis*: built by Newport News Shipbuilding & Dry Dock Company, Newport News, Virginia, 1932. 9,237 gross tons; 508 feet long; 72 feet wide. Steam turbines, twin screw. Service speed 18 knots. 450 cruise passengers.]

SECONDHAND CONVERSIONS (right).

In the late sixties and early seventies, there were an unusually high number of surplus, out-of-work passenger-cargo ships on the block, most of them British and French. They had lost their trade to the airlines and the shift to containerization. Many Greeks saw these ships, which were often available at reduced prices, as ideal candidates for conversion to cruise ships. The 4,500-ton *Delos* was owned by the Efthymiadis Lines, another rapidly expanding Greek passenger operator that would be later ruined by negligence (in this case, by the sinking in 1977 of the ferry *Heleanna,* which had been loaded unsafely). The *Delos (right, top)* had been built in the early fifties as the *Azemmour* for the French colonial run to West African ports out of Marseilles. Her owner was the Compagnie Navigation de Paquet, the forerunner of the present Paquet Lines. When later rebuilt by the Greeks, the ship looked quite different (all of her original cargo hatches, for example, were removed). She cruised out of Piraeus on seven-day voyages until the collapse of her owners. [Built by Ateliers et Chantiers de Bretagne, Nantes, France, 1951. 4,500 gross tons; 373 feet long; 49 feet wide. Steam turbines, single screw. Service speed 16 knots. 450 cruise passengers.]

Another former Frenchman, the *Tahitien* of 1953, continued her career with the Greeks. She had been a big combo liner, owned by Messageries Maritimes and used on the long-haul trade out of Marseilles to the South Pacific and Australia via the Caribbean and the Panama Canal. But in the end she too lost out to a rapidly diminishing passenger and cargo trade. In 1972 she went to the Greeks (to Aphrodite Cruises, which later became Mediterranean Sun Lines) as the *Atalante (right, middle).* She still runs regular two-week cruises out of Venice and has, perhaps, become even more successful financially in this second career. [Built by the Naval Dockyard, Brest, France, 1953. 12,614 gross tons; 549 feet long; 68 feet wide. Burmeister & Wain diesels, twin screw. Service speed 17 knots. 659 cruise passengers.]

The *La Palma* was another French colonial ship, the *Ferdinand de Lesseps,* which plied the old East African–Mauritius run out of Marseilles. She too was gutted and rebuilt for cruising, first sailing for Efthymiadis Lines in the late sixties as their *Delphi* and then joining the Cypriot-registered Intercruise Limited in 1977 as *La Palma (right, bottom).* She trades mostly in the Eastern Mediterranean and her clientele tends to be European vacationers. [Built by Chantiers de la Gironde, Bordeaux, France, 1952. 10,882 gross tons; 492 feet long; 64 feet wide. Burmeister & Wain–type diesels, twin screw. Service speed 17 knots. 790 cruise passengers.]

While these secondhand ships have often proved to be lucrative investments, they have, on occasion, been subject to some bad press: mechanical breakdowns, canceled sailings, poor sanitation reports, disgruntled, underpaid crewmen and, in one instance, the report that passengers had to make their own beds and serve their own meals!

The summer of 1986 was especially devastating to many of these firms, as it was to almost all those in Mediterranean service. Because of Libyan and Arab terrorism, the Lebanese war, airplane hijackings and the two-day capture of the *Achille Lauro,* business slumped to a point at which almost every Greek cruise ship was for sale. Well-known, popular ships such as the *Atlas, Jupiter, Orion* and *Aquarius* were laid up for the entire tourist season and two companies—Hellenic Mediterranean and the K Lines—collapsed from the financial strain.

AZURE SEAS (opposite).

Because of the dramatic increases in fuel-oil costs in the early seventies, many out-of-work liners were unable to find buyers. Consequently, many ships, often in adequate condition, went prematurely to the scrap heap. The 24,700-ton *Northern Star* of Britain's Shaw Savill Line was broken up at the age of 13! One of the exceptions was her smaller sister and former running mate, the *Southern Cross.* The first big liner of the fifties to have engines and her funnel mounted aft, she found a guardian angel in the Greek-flag Ulysses Line, which rebuilt her as the cruise ship *Calypso (opposite, top)* and sailed her in European and American waters. In 1980, she found another buyer, the Western Cruise Lines, which renamed her *Azure*

Seas for a new venture in West Coast cruising: twice-weekly three- and four-day cruises out of Los Angeles to Ensenada, Mexico (later expanded to include San Diego as well as Catalina Island). Her interiors have been modernized, her service and food are exemplary and her general popularity such that her future seems assured. The 370 crew members of the *Azure Seas,* some of whom are seen opposite, bottom, are similar to those found on most contemporary cruise ships. Her Greek master and Swedish deputy captain top off a staff that is comprised of over 25 different nationalities—Filipinos, Thais, Portuguese, Italians, Indonesians and Jamaicans, to name but a few. [Built by Harland & Wolff Limited, Belfast, Northern Ireland, 1955. 20,204 gross tons; 604 feet long; 78 feet wide. Steam turbines, twin screw. Service speed 20 knots. 732 cruise passengers.]

ANKARA (*opposite, top*).

One of the dowagers of "Med cruising" was Turkey's *Ankara*, a ship dating back to the twenties, when she sailed as the American intercoastal and cruising liner *Iroquois*. She went to the Turks after the Second World War and, although she was used primarily for interport services from Istanbul to Marseilles, Genoa (where she is seen here) and Naples, she also did considerable cruising. Usually, she carried British travelers. Under charter to Swan's Hellenic Cruises, she was known for detailed itineraries and a superb onboard lecture program, featuring such speakers as authors, archeologists and anthropologists. She served well into the seventies, perhaps past her best, but popular to the very end. Many of her passengers, apparently less concerned with the aged ship herself than with the ports of call, the overall travel experience, traveled aboard her year after year. A Greek ship, Epirotiki's *Orpheus*, currently maintains the Swan's program at sea. [Built by Newport News Shipbuilding & Dry Dock Company, Newport News, Virginia, 1927. 6,178 gross tons; 409 feet long; 62 feet wide. Steam turbines, twin screw. Service speed 18 knots. 406 cruise-passenger maximum.]

AMBASADOR (*opposite, bottom*).

The Yugoslavians have also dabbled in cruising, including a trio of ships that called at the many ports along the Adriatic coast and sometimes as far as Piraeus in Greece. These three sister ships, the *Jadran*, the *Jugoslavija* and the *Jedinstvo*, were fitted with quarters for 160 in first class, 30 or so tourist class and about 1,000 deck class (without berths). For many travelers, their services proved an inter-esting and unusual alternative in cruise travel. Later, however, when they were replaced by more efficient, high-capacity ferries, they were sold. The *Jadran* became a restaurant at Toronto; the *Jugoslavija* went to the Epirotiki Lines to run day cruises as the *Hermes*; and the *Jedinstvo* became the *Ambasador* for Atlas-Ambasador Cruises and has since divided her time between summers in the Mediterranean and winters in the Caribbean (the latter being more recently themed to "dive cruises"). Here she is calling at Istanbul. [Built by Brodogradilište, Split, Yugoslavia, 1958. 2,637 gross tons; 295 feet long; 45 feet wide. Sulzer diesels, twin screw. Service speed 18 knots. 206 cruise-passenger maximum.]

FUNCHAL (*above*).

Built for Portugal's Empresa Insulana for the colonial service from Lisbon out to Madeira and the Azores, the *Funchal* also served periodically as the national yacht. By 1972, her three-class quarters had been changed for one-class cruising and the original turbines were replaced by more efficient diesels. Used for cruises ever since (Scandinavian waters in the summers and South America in winter), she still is generally thought of as a Portuguese ship, although she flies the Panamanian flag and is owned by a combination of Portuguese, Swedish and Greek interests. She sails under the banner of a group known as Fritidskryss. In this view she is at Le Havre. [Built by Elsinore Shipbuilding & Engineering Company, Elsinore, Denmark, 1961. 9,824 gross tons; 501 feet long; 63 feet wide. Diesels, twin screw. Service speed 20 knots. Approximately 500 cruise passengers.]

ALEXANDER (above).

The little West German cruise ship *Regina Maris*, owned by the Lübeck Line, was well known for her unique itineraries: Spitzbergen, Iceland and the North Cape in summer; in the rest of the year around the British Isles, down to the remote parts of West Africa and farther afield (usually under special charter) to secluded ports in the Far East while sailing between Manila and Singapore. But her costly operations grew more and more troublesome. Put up for sale, she was intended to become a Caribbean gambling ship based at Santo Domingo. There was another plan to run her on the St. Lawrence River out of Montreal, perhaps even into the Great Lakes. But, in 1983, in a surprise announcement, she was sold to John S. Latsis, an extremely rich Greek shipping tycoon. While Latsis had owned passenger ships in the past, most he used for the austere Moslem pilgrim trades, so it was considered unlikely that he now wanted to enter the cruise trades. Renamed *Alexander*, honoring the first Latsis grandchild, the ship was sent to a West German shipyard, stripped and luxuriously rebuilt—but for only a dozen passengers. Mystery shrouded all other details. When she finally reached Greek waters, her future finally became clear: She was to be a gift from Latsis to the royal house of Saudi Arabia. Now, she is a luxurious "guest ship" for the family and their guests. Coincidentally, another Greek-owned passenger ship, Sun Line's original *Stella Solaris*, later became a yacht for a Middle Eastern sheik and at least two Chandris liners, the *Britanis* and the *Ariane*, served as temporary hotel and accommodation ships to the Saudi Arabian king and his family and friends. [Built by Lübecker Flenderwerke AG, Lübeck, West Germany, 1966. 5,813 gross tons; 390 feet long; 54 feet wide. Diesels, twin screw. Service speed 18 knots. 276 cruise passengers.]

THE SOVIETS (opposite, top).

The Soviets have amassed the largest passenger-ship fleet in the world (45 ships totaling 429,000 tons in 1988). It is usually divided into three major deep-sea groups: ships based in the Baltic, those on the Black Sea and those in the Far East. The state-owned ships are run at the discretion of the government to include both passenger services and military duties. The passenger-cruise services are divided into two operations: charters to the West (often through a specially created subsidiary, the so-called CTC Lines) and internal services for the Soviets themselves and such related passengers as Eastern Europeans. In Western services, these passenger ships have always been an important means of obtaining much-needed foreign currency. The ships have been chartered to the West Germans, the Dutch, the Italians, the Australians and, until the late seventies, the Americans and the Canadians. Certainly, the Soviet fleet has been very diverse.

The *Baltika*, shown here at Copenhagen (with the French *Mermoz* and another Soviet passenger ship, the *Mikhail Sholokhov*, behind her) was one of the most popular Soviet cruise ships. She was on the Baltic line, usually sailing from London to Copenhagen, sometimes to Stockholm or Helsinki, and then to Leningrad. This provided a very interesting round-trip voyage, especially in the peak summer season. Often, between her visits to London, she sailed across the Channel to Le Havre and back, offering a weekend mini-cruise. That the ship was Soviet, with its hints of secrecy and unusual food and entertainment, added to the fascination of such a short voyage. In fact, the food aboard Soviet passenger ships tended to be plentiful if not gourmet, the accommodations offering rather basic comforts and the entertainment often being provided by the crew.

The *Baltika*, special in her own right, had two historic distinctions in her career. In 1959, she brought Nikita Khrushchev across the Atlantic to New York for a United Nations meeting. Berthed at a nearby East River pier, she served as the hotel ship for the premier and his entourage. Then, 25 years later, she served again as an accommodation ship, this time for Mikhail Gorbachev and his staff during a summit conference with President Ronald Reagan at Reykjavík in Iceland. In the late eighties, because of several Soviet passenger-ship tragedies, all ships built prior to 1960, including the veteran *Baltika*, were marked for retirement. She finished her days far from her original trades, at a remote scrap yard at Gadāni Beach in Pakistan. [Built by the Netherlands Shipbuilding & Dry Dock Company, Amsterdam, The Netherlands, 1940. 7,494 gross tons; 445 feet long; 60 feet wide. Steam turbo-electric, twin screw. Service speed 16 knots. 437 passengers (77 first class, 360 tourist class).]

SOVIET CONVERSIONS FROM GERMAN SHIPS (opposite, bottom).

The Soviets acquired a good number of ex-German liners after the Second World War and, while many were either damaged or even sunk, their rehabilitation was well worth the effort. The largest of these, the 23,500-ton *Sovetsky Sojus* (meaning Soviet Union), the former Hamburg-America liner *Hansa* of the mid-twenties, was salvaged in 1950, but did not return to service for another five years. Another former member of the Hamburg-America prewar fleet, the *Iberia*, was seized in the summer of 1945, and renamed *Pobeda* (meaning victory). Used in the Black Sea coastal service, she sailed mostly between Odessa, Eupatoria, Yalta, Novorossisk, Sochi, Sukhumi and Batum. This was perhaps the most popular of all Soviet cruise services, and the many ships used on this run have often been filled to the last upper bunk. The passenger complements might include the Soviets themselves or Bulgarians or Romanians, Poles, Czechs and East Germans. Occasionally, there were

special longer voyages—perhaps with troops, technicians and laborers on board—to Egypt, East Africa, Indonesia and frequently to Cuba.

Another notable ex-German in Soviet hands was the *Admiral Nakhimov*. Built in 1925 as North German Lloyd's *Berlin*, she was cruising in the Black Sea when, on August 31, 1986, she and a Soviet freighter collided. The 61-year-old passenger ship sank within 20 minutes and 398 passengers and crew perished in the worst known peacetime Soviet maritime disaster. Months before, in February, one of the nation's finest liners, the *Mikhail Lermontov*, had sunk in New Zealand waters after striking a reef while on a cruise out of Sydney with a full load of Australians on board. Then, in the following November, a smaller passenger ship, the 5,000-ton *Turkmenia*, carrying 600 children, was seriously damaged by a fire at sea while off the Siberian coast. In the following year, a Soviet passenger ship burned at her berth in Kobe, Japan. Moscow suddenly saw ships built before 1960 as a risk and so all of them, including the last of those prewar Germans, went off to the wreckers. [*Pobeda*: built by Schichau Shipyards, Danzig, Germany, 1928. 9,828 gross tons; 505 feet long; 61 feet wide. Sulzer diesels, twin screw. Service speed 14.5 knots. 1,004 passengers (56 first class, 130 second class, 218 third class, 600 deck).]

MAXIM GORKY.

One of the most luxurious Soviet liners has been the *Maxim Gorky,*
built in the late sixties for the short-lived German Atlantic Line as
the *Hamburg.* Her career of long, luxurious trips was complicated
by the high costs of running a West German liner and also by the
unexpected high fuel-oil increases of 1973. She was put up for sale,
and it was said that the Japanese wanted her for interisland cruising out of Yokohama, but, through a special Liberian intermediary,
she went to the Soviets' Black Sea Shipping Company of Odessa.
Her first assignment was a short charter to United Artists Films,
who sent her up to the storm-tossed seas off Scotland, where, as the
temporarily renamed *Britannic,* she was used as the "floating set"
for the film *Juggernaut.* After she was briefly used in American
cruise service (1974–75), she was placed under a long-term charter
to the giant Neckermann Travel Company of Frankfurt. And so,
carrying a majority of German passengers (including a good number of capitalist millionaires), she has remained a German liner. Her
itineraries tend to take her to Scandinavia in the summer, the Mediterranean and Black Sea in fall and on an annual cruise around the
world (sometimes for as long as 150 days). It was during one of
these cruises, on June 28, 1989, that she made headline news when
she accidentally rammed Arctic pack ice during a voyage to the
North Cape and Spitzbergen. In danger of sinking, she revived
memories of the *Titanic.* Later, however, with her passengers removed and her hull temporarily patched, she was towed to the
naval base at Murmansk and later down to Bremerhaven for full
repairs (which cost $14 million). She resumed sailing, after day-
and-night shifts of repairs, in mid-August. In December, she was
again in the news: She was the setting for a summit meeting between Premier Mikhail Gorbachev and President George Bush.
Many of the reporters who came aboard were surprised by her
luxurious interiors. One referred to her style as "Soviet deco."
[Built by Deutsche Werft, Hamburg, West Germany, 1969. 24,981
gross tons; 642 feet long; 90 feet wide. Steam turbines, twin screw.
Service speed 23.5 knots. 790 cruise-passenger maximum.]

SOVIET EXPANSION.

In the sixties, the Soviets, deciding on large, deep-sea expansion of their passenger fleet, contracted an East German shipyard to build five sister and near-sister ships: the *Ivan-Franko* (1964), the *Alexandr Pushkin* (1965), the *Taras Schevchenko* (1967), the *Shota Rustavelli* (1968) and the *Mikhail Lermontov* (1972). These were designed with improved quarters and extra amenities for overseas services—transatlantic crossings to Montreal and New York, cruises from London, Rotterdam, Bremerhaven, Genoa and even far-off Sydney, tourist voyages to Australia and periodic trips around the world (which were sold both as full cruises and in port-to-port segments). Otherwise, they might occasionally show up on the Black Sea coastal run or cross to Havana with students. To this date (1990), these 20,000-tonners still rank as the largest newly built Soviet passenger ships. In recent years, they have been upgraded with better facilities, improved decor, additional private bathrooms in the cabins and a change to tropical white hulls (they had been painted in black when built). The *Mikhail Lermontov (left, top)* was perhaps the most lavishly redecorated, as seen in views of her main lounge *(left, middle)* and the sitting room of a suite *(left, bottom)*. Shown departing from Tilbury, the port for London, she was later reassigned to Australian cruise service. On February 16, 1986, while on one of these trips, she struck the rocks near New Zealand's South Island, began to flood and then sank. The Soviets were both saddened and embarrassed at the loss of one of their finest and largest liners. [Built by Mathias-Thesen Werft Shipyard, Wismar, East Germany, 1972. 19,872 gross tons; 578 feet long; 77 feet wide; 27-foot draft. Sulzer diesels, twin screw. Service speed 20 knots. Approximately 700 cruise passengers.]

THE CHINESE (above).

Until very recently, the Chinese passenger fleet has been veiled in secrecy. But with little information available to the West, whole fleets of smaller passenger ships have been built for river and coastal trading. These so-called "internal services" are offered only to nationals. However, since the sixties, the Chinese have acquired some secondhand deep-sea passenger tonnage, often for a variety of reasons. The former French *Ancerville*, for example, which became the *Minghua*, worked a trade out to East Africa, carrying technicians and work crews for a Tanzanian railway-building project before being upgraded and then shifted to Australian charter-cruise service. Others, such as the *Jinjiang*, (formerly the American cruise ship *Mariposa*) and the *Shanghai*, the ex-*Cathay* of P & O, run regular cruises between Hong Kong and Shanghai. Still another, the *Ziluolan*, the former Japanese industrial trade-display ship *Sakura Maru*, runs a more eclectic balance of short trips over to Hong Kong and down to Singapore, others out to the Pacific islands and occasional long hauls to Australia. [Built by Mitsubishi Heavy Industries Limited, Kobe, Japan, 1962. 12,628 gross tons; 511 feet long; 69 feet wide. Mitsubishi-Sulzer diesel, single screw. Service speed 17 knots. Approximately 950-passenger maximum.]

EXPEDITION CRUISES (opposite).

For the very experienced cruise traveler, one of the increasingly popular options is "expedition cruises." Run aboard specially built, usually small cruisers, their amenities are special too—heated crow's-nest observatories, hulls strengthened to withstand ice, lecture rooms, extensive libraries and Zodiacs (inflatable rafts that land passengers in almost-inaccessible locations such as the Arctic ice pack or a deserted Indian Ocean island beach). The entertainment, less of the customary cruise-ship fare, consists of bird-watching, nature walks on shore (meeting the Antarctic penguins being perhaps best known) and lectures on such topics as saving the whales, glaciers and tribal customs.

Lindblad Travel pioneered these trips as commercial cruise travel in the late sixties with their specially built *Lindblad Explorer*. But she now sails for a competitor, Society Expeditions, as the *Society Explorer (opposite, top)*. Generally, she divides her time between winters in the Antarctic and summers along the Alaskan coast, the Canadian Arctic and Maritimes, and across to Greenland. Her running mate, the slightly larger *World Discoverer (opposite, bottom)*, also spends the December–March period in the Antarctic (where she is seen in a dramatic setting), but then sails in Far Eastern, East Indian and South Pacific waters for the remainder of the year. [*Society Explorer*: built by Nystad Varv Shipyard, Helsinki, Finland, 1969. 2,500 gross tons; 250 feet long; 46 feet wide. Diesel, single screw. Service speed 13 knots. 100 cruise passengers. *World Discoverer*: built by Schichau Shipyard, Bremerhaven, West Germany, 1974. 3,153 gross tons; 279 feet long; 49 feet wide. M.A.K. diesels, twin screw. Service speed 16 knots. 136 cruise passengers.]

RIVER CRUISING.

River cruising has become increasingly popular: the Amazon, the Rhine, the Danube and the Volga, the Nile and the Mississippi (and its tributaries). Specialty craft usually serve these areas—ships with shallower draft, or wider and flatter hulls. The New Orleans–based Delta Queen Steamboat Company has two of the very best, the newer *Mississippi Queen* (left), more like a cruise ship, and the older, more traditional *Delta Queen* (right). The older ship is something of a national treasure and, despite her advanced age and worries over her safety, she receives constant exemptions from the regulatory authorities.

The ships put into a long list of historically evocative ports:

Baton Rouge, Natchez, Pittsburgh and St. Paul. On-board entertainment and fare are appropriate: Dixieland jazz, mint juleps, mud pie and, on deck, a steam pipe organ. They create a cruise experience that might just be the best trip back in time. [*Mississippi Queen:* built by Jeffboat, Inc., Jeffersonville, Indiana, 1976. 4,500 gross tons; 379 feet long; 68 feet wide. Compound condensing engine, paddlewheel. Service speed approximately 7 knots. 500 cruise-passenger maximum. *Delta Queen:* assembled at Stockton, California, 1926. 1,837 gross tons; 285 feet long; 58 feet wide. Cross compound condensing engine, paddlewheel. Service speed approximately 5 knots. 186 passengers.]

END OF THE *LAVIA*.

Despite their overall glamour, their increased operational sophistication and stringent inspections and surveys by local authorities, cruise ships must still contend with storms and fogs, collisions, groundings and—a vulnerability particular to older, converted ships—fire. Some sink during fires, having been overloaded with fire fighters' water while others, scorched and corpselike, are deemed to be "beyond economic repair" by company engineers and insurance underwriters.

The Hong Kong–owned, Panamanian-registered *Lavia* is one of the more extreme recent examples. She had been lying about Hong Kong harbor for years when, in January 1989, a fire broke out, spread quickly and did extensive damage (*above*). Attended to by a small flotilla of fireboats, she soon became top-heavy and rolled over (*left*). Now the situation necessitated a tediously long and expensive salvage. Once righted, however, inspections revealed that the damages were extreme, especially in light of her advanced age of 42. The nearby scrap yards of Kaohsiung on Taiwan proved to be her final destination.

The *Lavia* had been a Cunard transatlantic passenger ship, the combination-style *Media* on the Liverpool–New York run, until sold, in 1961–62, to be rebuilt for the Australian immigrant trade as the Italian-owned *Flavia*. She was made into a cruise ship in 1968 and, under the Costa Line banner, sailed on the overnight runs between Florida and the Bahamas. In 1982 she was sold (with faltering turbines) to Chinese interests, but thereafter became a "mystery ship." She was renamed *Flavian* and then *Lavian*, and periodic rumors of reactivation as a cruise ship never materialized. Instead, her only voyages seemed to be very short ones: shifting from one Hong Kong anchorage to another. [Built by John Brown & Company Limited, Clydebank, Scotland, 1947. 15,465 gross tons; 556 feet long; 70 feet wide. Steam turbines, twin screw. Service speed 18 knots. 1,120 cruise-passenger maximum.]

THE SCRAPPERS.

Most older cruise ships meet with far less dramatic endings at the hands of the scrappers. First stripped of a few selected keepsakes by their owners and the odd, resellable item by the scrappers, the hulls, their upper decks empty, lounges deserted and staterooms lifeless, go off, usually under the guidance of a tug or two, to quiet, backwater berths where they are cut down and then gradually dragged ashore until the final pieces are cut up. At crowded berths at the port of Kaohsiung, the Taiwanese have been the busiest scrappers in recent years (over 100 passenger ships alone in the past 20 years). But they now have serious competitors in the dismantling firms at Aliağa in Turkey and Gadāni Beach in Pakistan.

The Chandris cruise ship *Regina Prima (right, top)* nears her end at Aliağa. She is offshore and already much of her bow section has been cut down to the waterline. One lifeboat remains in place near the stern, yet her funnel appears to have no evident signs of her long neglect in lay up near Piraeus. Having been the American cruise ships *Panama* and *President Hoover* in prior careers, she had reached the age of 46. [Built by Bethlehem Steel Company, Quincy, Massachusetts, 1939. 10,603 gross tons; 493 feet long; 64 feet wide. Steam turbines, twin screw. Service speed 17.5 knots. 600 cruise passengers.]

In a view of July 20, 1982 *(right, middle)*, two passenger ships are systematically being hauled ashore. Work is already well under way on the former Mediterranean cruise ship *Ankara* (then 55 years old) and is soon to begin on the far newer coastal passenger-cargo ship *Iskenderun*. Both ships were well-known members of the Turkish Maritime Lines. [*Iskenderun:* built by S. A. Ansaldo Shipyards, Genoa, Italy, 1950. 6,570 gross tons; 433 feet long; 57 feet wide; 18-foot draft. Steam turbines, twin screw. Service speed 16.5 knots. 416 passengers (25 deluxe, 71 first class, 320 tourist class).]

Another Mediterranean cruise ship, the Greek-owned *Bella Maria (right, bottom;* former French *Azemmour* and then the Efthymiadis Lines' *Delos)* was not quite as fortunate in reaching the scrappers. Laid up for some years near Piraeus, she was about to leave for the breakers when she grounded in an outer harbor. Photographed in June 1988 in Piraeus Roads, she remained in position for some time, rusting further and all but completely abandoned. Finally, she was pulled free and then went off to the breakers. [Built by Ateliers et Chantiers de Bretagne, Nantes, France, 1951. 3,921 gross tons; 373 feet long; 49 feet wide. 22-foot draft. Steam turbines, single screw. Service speed 16 knots. 266 passengers (56 first class, 46 second class, and 164 dormitory).]

The Early Eighties: Renaissance

IN MARCH 1977 a crowd had assembled on the rooftop of Berth 2 of New York's new Consolidated Passenger Ship Terminal, located along the once-busy West Side transatlantic-liner piers. We looked across to the sparkling white hull of the newest liner in the world, the 17,000-ton *Cunard Princess*. An excursion boat had been specially brought in and wedged between the new ship's bow and the pier. Its top deck served as a stage from which the liner would be christened—the first time a cruise ship had been so named at New York. A small army of reporters and photographers had come out for the occasion. Princess Grace of Monaco had consented to do the honors. The champagne bottle smashed over the bow as planned and the crowd cheered.

But there was one discouraging note: Some industry analysts were saying that the entire cruise industry had peaked, reached its saturation point, and, furthermore, that the *Cunard Princess* would probably be the last new cruise ship. In fact, the overall situation was not as bright or as encouraging as it had been a few years before. Fuel-oil prices had jumped from $35 to $95 a ton. Even when full to the very last upper berth, some ships could no longer return a profit. Some shipowners foundered.

Shortly after the *Cunard Princess* entered service, however, there was a gradual and then a marked improvement. More and more travelers were seeing cruises as excellent value. By 1979, many companies, while ready for further expansion, were still unwilling to build new tonnage. Two alternatives were demonstrated by the conversion of the *France/Norway* and the "stretching" of the Royal Caribbean Cruise and Royal Viking liners.

Even greater growth followed. Finally, shipowners were willing to gamble. They asked for bids from shipbuilders for so-called "newbuildings"—ships that were still larger. In the early 1980s, we come to the high-pitch, state-of-the-art *Song of America*, the *Europa*, the sisters *Nieuw Amsterdam* and *Noordam*, the *Fairsky* and the *Royal Princess*. We also see the creation of specialty ships for the ultra-luxury market, the *Sea Goddess* "yachts" and other developments such as the increasing size of Carnival Cruise Line's so-called "mega-cruiseships."

CONVERSION OF THE *FRANCE*.

Following the dramatic, devastating fuel-oil increases of 1973–74, international passenger shipping fell into a slump. Recovery seemed distant. In fact, in 1977, when Cunard added its 17,500-ton *Cunard Princess,* some analysts said that she would be the last new cruise ship to be built for some years to come. Others actually forecast that the cruise industry had reached its peak—realized maximum of its potential. But within a year or so, such farsighted firms as Norwegian Caribbean Lines were seeking additional tonnage, even bigger ships than they had owned previously, seeing the future as a boom period. The possibilities for expansion were unlimited. However, company directors were reluctant to build new ships and, instead, surveyed laid-up tonnage as well as other ships on the sales lists. In particular, they looked over the idle *United States,* the sister ships *Michelangelo* and *Raffaello,* and then, biggest of all, the *France.* In the end, it was the last-named ship, withdrawn from transatlantic service in 1974 and quietly lying at a Le Havre backwater berth *(left),* that was chosen. Underwritten by the de Gaulle government and completed in the early sixties, she had been, it was said, built to last for 50 years. Everything about her was of the highest standard.

Norwegian Caribbean Lines bought the *France* for $18 million (she had cost $80 million to build nearly 20 years before) and, in August 1979, moved her to the Hapag-Lloyd Shipyards at Bremerhaven for the biggest conversion of the time *(above).* Within a year and at an overall cost of $130 million, she was completely "transformed" from the indoor, transatlantic *France* to the outdoor, tropical *Norway.* [Built by Chantiers de l'Atlantique, St. Nazaire, France, 1961. 70,202 gross tons; 1,035 feet long; 110 feet wide. Steam turbines, twin screw. Service speed 16 knots. 2,181 cruise-passenger maximum.]

Conversion of the France. Work on the ship was extensive *(above, left)*. The *France*'s class-divided quarters were reshaped, redecorated and certainly updated. In their place, a whole new floating, fun-in-the-sun resort was created: two outdoor pools and vast sunning and lido decks, an open-air restaurant and a basketball court, two decks of shops, a disco (with neon-lighted, Plexiglas flooring), a huge casino and an ice cream parlor. Even the twin-level theater was refitted, and it featured Las Vegas cabarets and Broadway shows. Even the enormous hull (she is the longest passenger ship ever to put to sea) was brought down to its original steel and then redone in a handsome navy. The unique winged funnels were repainted as well, the French red and black giving way to Norwegian Caribbean's blues and white *(above, right)*. One of her two original engine rooms was closed down to reduce costs and the crew was cut from 1,100 to 800. In fact, so diverse were the nationalities of her cruise staff and crew (over 25 countries being represented) that the *Norway* flew the United Nations flag as well as the Norwegian colors.

NORWAY.

Delivered in May 1980, the *Norway* made a celebratory transatlantic crossing to New York as part of her reintroduction to service. She sailed early the morning after her arrival and passed the inbound *Queen Elizabeth 2* (Hoboken is in the background). It was the first meeting in some time of the two largest liners afloat. But almost at the very same time, there were boardroom discussions and initial plans for even bigger cruise ships. The renaissance was beginning.

In her first years, the *Norway* settled down successfully on the weekly Miami–Caribbean circuit, sailing only to St. Thomas and a Bahamian out island, affording her passengers additional time at sea.

LENGTHENING SHIPS.

In the late seventies other cruise firms were equally cautious about so-called "new-buildings," looking instead at existing tonnage. Two of them opted to lengthen ships in their fleets. The Royal Caribbean Cruise Line sister ships *Song of Norway* and *Nordic Prince (below)*, were returned to their Finnish builders in 1978 and 1980 respectively, cut in half and fitted with 85-foot midsections. This increased their overall capacities from 724 to 1,040, in anticipation of the "cruise boom" of the eighties. Amazingly, the entire process was completed on each ship in little more than three months. [*Nordic Prince:* built by Wärtsilä Shipyards, Helsinki, Finland, 1971. 23,200 gross tons; 644 feet long; 78 feet wide. Wärtsilä-Sulzer diesels, twin screw. Service speed 21 knots. 1,040 cruise passengers.]

Another Norwegian firm, the Royal Viking Line, decided to expand as well by "stretching" their three deluxe cruise ships. At the Hapag-Lloyd yards at Bremerhaven, each was given a 90-foot insertion, increasing the capacity of each from 536 to 758. The *Royal Viking Sea*, the last to be altered, is seen on these pages in March 1983. The new midsection has just been moved into the slip and is temporarily secured to the existing stern section while the forward piece is about to be returned to position. [Built by Wärtsilä Shipyards, Helsinki, Finland, 1973. 28,221 gross tons; 674 feet long; 83 feet wide. Wärtsilä-Sulzer diesels, twin screw. Service speed 21 knots. 758 cruise-passenger maximum.]

SONG OF AMERICA.

Soon after "jumboizing" the *Song of Norway* and *Nordic Prince*, the Royal Caribbean Cruise Lines found that it needed still more berths to meet demands. But now it was ready to gamble with a new ship. It returned to the acclaimed Wärtsilä Shipyards at Helsinki and ordered one of the biggest new cruise ships of that period, the 37,500-ton *Song of America* (*above*). Delivered in November 1982, she was assigned to one of the busiest cruise itineraries of all, sailing out of Miami to the eastern Caribbean—seven days to Nassau, San Juan and St. Thomas. She was later reassigned to the alternate western Caribbean run and is shown moored at Ocho Rios on Jamaica.

The ship's design represented over ten years of Royal Caribbean experience and resulted in, among other features, an exceptional layout of her public rooms. Nearly all of these were conveniently located on two decks. The two dining rooms (one of which is shown opposite, top) were only one deck below the main lounges, lounges with stages, shops, bars and card room (*opposite, bottom*). Twin-bedded cabins (*opposite, middle*), quite compact, represented the philosophy of cruise-ship operators and designers that passengers actually spent little time in their staterooms. The ship was fitted with one of the largest upper-deck pools yet to go to sea. In addition to the two oversized pools, there was seating for over 1,000 passengers in reclining chairs. [Built by Wärtsilä Shipyards, Helsinki, Finland, 1982. 37,584 gross tons; 703 feet long; 93 feet wide. Wärtsilä-Sulzer diesels, twin screw. Service speed 21 knots. 1,575 cruise-passenger maximum.]

EUROPA.

West Germany's Hapag-Lloyd began a series of tests for a new cruise ship in the seventies. With a 70 percent repeat rate among passengers and an inner circle of German millionaires, a high-standard liner was a necessity. Designs were approved for the *Europa* *(above)*, one of the most luxurious liners of the eighties, shown sailing up the Hudson River in New York. Averaging about 600 passengers per cruise, her on-board ambience is that of a big yacht, as seen in views of her pool *(opposite, top)* and one of her lounges *(opposite, bottom)*.

The original plan was to divide the government-subsidized construction between two different shipyards and join the two parts, giving work to two important political constituencies. This novel scheme never came to pass; instead the ship was built entirely at Bremen. [Built by Bremer-Vulkan Shipyard, Bremen, West Germany, 1981. 33,819 gross tons; 655 feet long; 92 feet wide. M.A.N. diesels, twin screw. Service speed 21 knots. 758 cruise-passenger maximum.]

NIEUW AMSTERDAM.

The Holland-America Line added two new liners to their fleet. The *Nieuw Amsterdam* (shown above arriving at New York in July 1983) and the *Noordam* have been appraised as two of the most beautifully decorated liners of their day. They are floating treasure chests of art and antiques, all of which are blended in very advanced and contemporary liners.

The *Nieuw Amsterdam*'s decoration, for example, takes as its theme the exploration of the Dutch West India Company in the New World—with paintings, maps and documents, murals, painted tiles, statues, china, weapons and armor, historic costumes and old navigational instruments. Highlights include a reproduc-

tion of the document confirming the original Dutch purchase of the island of Manhattan and a fully detailed model of Henry Hudson's *Half Moon*. Other decorative touches include a Venetian lantern from 1580, Chinese Ming plates and a seventeenth-century Dutch wedding chest. The main lounge is shown opposite.

The *Nieuw Amsterdam* and *Noordam* ply Alaskan waters in the summer, sailing out of Vancouver on weekly trips; they are in Caribbean waters for the remainder of the year. [*Nieuw Amsterdam:* built by Chantiers de l'Atlantique, St. Nazaire, France, 1983. 33,930 gross tons; 704 feet long; 90 feet wide. Sulzer diesels, twin screw. Service speed 21 knots. 1,210 cruise passengers.]

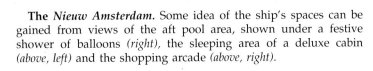

The *Nieuw Amsterdam.* Some idea of the ship's spaces can be gained from views of the aft pool area, shown under a festive shower of balloons *(right)*, the sleeping area of a deluxe cabin *(above, left)* and the shopping arcade *(above, right).*

FAIRSKY.

By 1980, Monte Carlo–based Sitmar Cruises wanted to expand their American West Coast operations. Through one of their Panamanian-registered subsidiaries, the Fairline Shipping Company, they bought the 19,300-ton *Príncipe Perfeito* of 1961. She had been used until 1976 in the Portuguese-African colonial trades; then, with other Panama-flag owners, she had served as the Middle Eastern hotel ship *Al Hasa*. Sitmar planned to rebuild her lavishly as the *Fairsky*. However, there was some rethinking and the ship was laid up under the temporary name *Vera*. A brand-new *Fairsky* was ordered from the French, at a cost of over $150 million. She is shown departing from Los Angeles on her maiden voyage, a cruise to the Mexican Riviera, in May 1984. The *Vera* never became a Sitmar liner. In 1982, she was sold to Greek buyers and soon returned to the Middle East for further service as a workers' accommodation ship. [*Fairsky:* built by CNIM Shipyards, La Seyne, France, 1984. 46,314 gross tons; 790 feet long; 90 feet wide. Steam turbines, twin screw. Service speed 19 knots. 1,212 cruise passengers.]

ROYAL PRINCESS.

Unquestionably, Princess Cruises' *Royal Princess* is another of the outstanding cruise liners of her time. Her design, her decor, her overall style place her in the very top class of all contemporary passenger ships.

The eight-deck *Royal Princess* was built by the renowned, highly productive Wärtsilä Marine Shipyard of Finland. She was com-

pleted at its Helsinki plant in October 1984 (and is shown above, top, in aerial photograph while fitting out, between the little *Sea Goddess II* and the big Baltic ferry *Mariella*). A month later, in November, she was sent to Southampton (London is, in fact, her home port) for christening by the Princess of Wales (seen touring the bridge, above, bottom).

The $165 million *Royal Princess* is a truly state-of-the-art ship. The

150-seat Princess Theatre *(above, bottom),* is located on the port side of the ship's Caribe Deck and the Crown Casino, with 102 one-arm bandits and tables for roulette, blackjack and craps *(above, top),* is a deck below, on the Riviera Deck. [Built by Wärtsilä Marine Shipyards, Helsinki, Finland, 1984. 44,348 gross tons; 761 feet long; 96 feet wide. Wärtsilä-Pielstick diesels, twin screw. Service speed 22 knots. 1,260 cruise passengers.]

The _Royal Princess._ The Plaza area (on Plaza Deck), for example, is spectacular, a circular space with a three-deck-high well and twin staircases. The central focus is a stainless-steel-and-bronze sculpture entitled _Spindrift._ Rising out of a bubbling rock-garden pool, it ranks as the most expensive item (over $300,000) in the ship's specially commissioned art collection (ceramics, enamels, tapestries, murals and lithographs).

92   _The Early Eighties: Renaissance_

The *Royal Princess.* The Lido Deck includes the ship's finest accommodations, two luxury suites, which might more aptly be called penthouses. The Royal Suite *(above, bottom)* and the Princess Suite *(above, top)* were planned down to such details as individual postal sleeves for shipboard mail deliveries. The Aloha and Baja decks are devoted to cabins and include 152 deluxe rooms with private terraces.

SEA GODDESS CRUISES (opposite).

The luxury, $600-a-day market for cruising was thought to have considerable possibilities for expansion in the eighties. Norwegian investors created the first of these ventures, the Sea Goddess Cruises, with the intention of building as many as eight 4,200-ton deluxe cruising yachts. Though this $2.5 billion plan was later modified and the number of ships reduced to two, the original concept persisted: great luxury blended with intimacy and specialization.

Commissioned in 1984–85, the sisters *Sea Goddess I* and *Sea Goddess II* (the former shown opposite, top, at Copenhagen with the *Arkona, Estonia* and *Ocean Princess*) represented a new generation of cruise vessels that offer a select atmosphere as well as the ability to visit smaller, more remote ports of call. The ships have a maximum capacity of 116 passengers berthed in 58 suites or double-berth rooms. Being among the most expensive cruise ships (a $6300 minimum fare for ten nights in 1986), their quarters are luxurious, as can be seen from a view of the main lounge–night club (*opposite, bottom*). All cabins have sitting rooms, for example, that can easily be converted into private dining rooms. Each stateroom has its own library, stereo system, television and VCR units, a snack-filled refrigerator, a fully stocked bar, wall safe and large wardrobes. Both *Sea Goddess* yachts—which came under Cunard management in 1986—roam to ports all over the world. [*Sea Goddess I:* built by Wärtsilä Shipyards, Helsinki, Finland, 1984. 4,200 gross tons; 344 feet long; 58 feet wide. Diesel, twin screw. Service speed 18 knots. 116 cruise passengers.]

CARNIVAL CRUISE LINES (above).

In 1972, Carnival Cruise Lines of Miami started up its Caribbean operations with a secondhand liner, the former *Empress of Canada,* which had been renamed *Mardi Gras.* In 1980, Carnival ordered the first of its new, specially designed ships, the 36,674-ton *Tropicale,* which came from Danish builders. The entire industry marveled at Carnival's success. But could it last? The *Tropicale* with her winged funnel and the likes of the Boiler Room Bar and the Exta-Z Disco, was the prototype for not one but a trio of "mega-liners": the 46,052-ton *Holiday,* added in July 1985; the 47,262-ton *Jubilee,* added in July 1986; and the 47,200-ton *Celebration,* added in March 1988. More additions were to follow. Yet another threesome was planned —bigger and more extravagant still: the 70,000-ton *Fantasy* and her two sisters, the *Ecstasy* and *Sensation.* Like all Carnival ships, their names evoke a party, the upbeat, fun-fun-fun!

The nine-deck *Celebration* and *Jubilee* ranked for a time as the fifth largest cruise ships afloat (only the *Sovereign of the Seas, Norway, QE2* and *Star Princess* were larger). Furthermore, while many noted cruise ships have come from Finland, the two ships are also of Scandinavian construction, but from Sweden, from the now-defunct Kockums yard at Malmö. The *Holiday* was created in nearby Denmark and holds the record for that nation. [*Celebration* and *Jubilee:* built by Kockums Shipyard, Malmö, Sweden, 1986 and 1987. 47,200 gross tons; 733 feet long; 94 feet wide. Sulzer diesels, twin screw. Service speed 22 knots. 1,850-passenger maximum.]

Carnival Cruise Lines. Carnival is the biggest and busiest cruise company in the world. In 1990, it had eight liners, totaling over 320,000 tons and 13,000 berths. In the summer of 1988, the company made an unsuccessful bid to take over the Royal Caribbean–Admiral Cruises Group, which would have meant an additional eight liners, including the world's largest, the 73,100-ton *Sovereign of the Seas*. Undaunted, Carnival moved quickly in other directions and in January, bought the upscale Holland-America Line operations, which also included Windstar Sail Cruises, adding another seven passenger ships. Carnival was also interested (although the idea now seems to be shelved) in the "Tiffany Project," a joint venture with Swedish interests for a trio of 48,000-tonners. The same size as the 1,850-passenger *Jubilee (opposite, top)* and her sister ships, these would carry nearly two-thirds fewer passengers, about 700, all of them in suites. According to initial projections, the first was to appear in 1992, and would be aimed at the Mediterranean market.

Ted Arison, the founder of Carnival, was listed (in 1989) as one of the 100 richest men in America, with a fortune placed at $1.6 billion. Other Arison interests include the Crystal Palace & Casino in the Bahamas, the largest hotel (1,500 rooms) in the Caribbean area; ownership in a bank, a Miami basketball team, a share in the Miami Sea Aquarium, condominiums, an office building and an airline called Carnival Air.

Long afternoon naps in a deck chair, drinks around the pool and outdoor games have turned the open upper decks of cruise ships into popular shipboard locations. Among the "newbuildings," decks have become expansive and uncluttered, and often include uniquely shaped pools and lido areas. Aboard Carnival's *Holiday* the forward swimming pool includes a 30-foot serpentine slide *(above)*. Neatly placed about are vinyl-and-metal recliners, which have replaced wooden deck chairs. The decking on board, however, remains traditional. Of Burmese teak, it covers two acres. [Built at Aalborg Vaerft Shipyard, Aalborg, Denmark, 1985. 46,052 gross tons; 725 feet long; 92 feet wide. Sulzer diesels, twin screw. Service speed 22 knots. 1,760 cruise passengers.]

The extraordinary Atlantis Lounge *(opposite, bottom)*, the main public room aboard Carnival's *Jubilee*, has seating for 900 on six levels and terraces. The seating itself is often varied: sofas, loveseats, banquettes, tables for two, even sections of theater-style pull-down seats. Twelve-foot-high golden seahorses, straight off the set of *Raiders of the Lost Ark*, flank the large main stage. The ceiling is done in copper, brass and stainless steel; the lighting snakes around in a horseshoe configuration; and the lighted artwork along the walls is in the geometric style of the Deco era's Aztec Airways. It is one of the most flamboyant, exceptional spaces ever to put to sea.

SCANDINAVIA.

A more experimental ship was the 26,748-ton *Scandinavia*. When completed in the summer of 1982, she ranked as the largest cruise ship–ferry yet built. Owned by Scandinavian World Cruises, a newly formed arm of the big DFDS Group of Copenhagen, her purpose was innovative: to carry passengers and their cars between New York and Florida. Unfortunately, being registered in the Bahamas and therefore lacking the required American registry to sail directly between two U.S. ports, she had to detour to Freeport in the Bahamas, where passengers disembarked and their cars were unloaded to be transferred to one of two smaller ferries, which then sailed to Miami or Port Canaveral. The venture was doomed to quick failure. In little more than a year, the *Scandinavia* was recalled by her Danish owners and placed on their overnight runs between Copenhagen and Oslo. Within another year or so, she was put up for sale. After some alterations, she became the *Stardancer* for the Seattle-based Sundance Cruises. [Built by Dubigeon-Normandie SA, Nantes, France, 1981. 26,748 gross tons; 610 feet long; 90 feet wide. Burmeister & Wain diesels, twin screw. Service speed 20 knots. 1,606 maximum passengers.]

QUEEN ELIZABETH 2.

In May 1982, the *Queen Elizabeth 2* once again made headline news around the world when she was called to duty by the British government to serve as a transport in the Falklands War. In the weeks that followed, she was featured in many news stories, including reports that the Argentines were desperately trying to sink her. Fortunately, she returned home safely. That August, fully repaired, her hull newly painted dove-gray (this was soon to prove impractical as the original black kept bleeding through), and wearing, for the first time in her career, the traditional Cunard funnel colors of orange-red and black, she was given heroic receptions in several ports. In this view, she is making a triumphant return to New York.

But there would be still more headlines: more extravagant accommodations for her celebrated around-the-world cruises, an expensive charter for New York's Liberty Weekend in July 1986, and then an extensive, $162 million conversion from steam turbine to diesel-electric (done at Bremerhaven over a six-month period beginning in October 1987). More recently, there were two long Japanese charters (at $625,000 per day), that saw the liner berthed at Yokohama, serving as a hotel and shopping center.

EXPLORATION CRUISE LINES *(opposite, top)*.

The smaller cruise ship has definite merits. Certainly, it differs from the larger, fun-in-the-sun, disco style of other liners. Instead, it is more yachtlike in tone. The main lounge, for example, is more akin to a large living room or club sitting room. The staff seems to know everyone by name and a sense of friendliness, of informality and relaxation, of "sit back and enjoy the trip" prevails. And because these ships usually call in at more remote, less-accessible ports, there is also a strong sense of adventure, of mental and visual stimulation—perhaps a purer kind of cruise travel.

Seattle-based Exploration Cruise Lines was created in 1972, and first concentrated on very small, bow-landing-type cruisers. But by 1984, in rather high-spirited expansion, the company began its "Starship class." A charter agreement was reached with Fearnley & Eger, Norwegian shippers best known for their cargo fleet, to operate two small deep-sea cruise ships: the 3,095-ton *North Star* and, in 1986, the 8,282-ton *Explorer Starship*. The latter spent her summers on the Alaskan run, sailing out of Prince Rupert in British Columbia, and her winters in the Caribbean, on weekly runs between San Juan and Barbados. In the photograph she is at Glacier Bay.

Exploration was forced into bankruptcy in 1988, and ships such as the *Explorer Starship*, which had been converted from a small container–cargo ship for cruising, had to find alternative employment. She was eventually sold to the Japanese, who now sail her as the *Song of Flower*, in Alaska in summer and on cruises from Singapore for the remainder of the year. [Built by Kristiansand Shipyards AS, Kristiansand, Norway, 1974; rebuilt for cruising 1985–86. 8,282 gross tons; 407 feet long; 52 feet wide. Diesels, twin screw. Service speed 16 knots. 250 cruise passengers.]

NORTH STAR *(opposite, bottom)*.

Another of Exploration's charter cruise ships was the small *North Star*, a converted fishing trawler. Of particular note was her ice-strengthened hull. Fully converted in 1983, she was renamed *North Star* (having been the *Marburg* and then the *Lindmar*) and was operated for a short time by the North Star Cruises for European cruising—primarily to the Norwegian fjords and the Mediterranean. She seemed the ideal charter for Exploration. Her small, cozy style made her the perfect vessel for adventure–explorer cruising; her

size and maneuverability were suitable to small ports. She cruised to Alaska during the summer, Baja California (where she is seen here) and other ports of Mexico in the off season. [Built by A/G Weser Shipyards, Bremerhaven, West Germany, 1966; rebuilt for cruising in 1983. 3,095 gross tons; 295 feet long; 46 feet wide. Diesel, single screw. Service speed 13.5 knots. 156 cruise-passenger maximum.]

PEARL OF SCANDINAVIA *(above)*.

In June 1982, Pearl Cruises began year-round operation in the Far East, becoming one of the pioneers in China cruising for Western passengers. Its parent, the Lauritzen Group of Denmark, saw a promising future for cruise services in this area and decided to make the gamble. (The Danes, with another well-known shipper, the East Asiatic Company, had had satisfactory experiences with the Chinese.) Headquartered at San Francisco, Pearl was a specially created cruise-operating subsidiary; the ship itself, the 12,456-ton *Pearl of Scandinavia* (renamed *Ocean Pearl* in 1988 after being bought by Ocean Cruise Lines), was registered in the Bahamas, an increasingly common flag of convenience. The ship was staffed with Danish officers, an international cruise staff and Filipinos in the hotel and deck departments. Pearl Cruises felt that cruise travelers, particularly Americans seeking a more enriching, more culturally exciting voyage, were prepared to make the long, often tiring connecting journeys by air. Ports of embarkation included Hong Kong, Singapore, Inchon and Yokohama. The gamble succeeded so that, by 1987, a quarter of the *Pearl's* passengers were repeaters. In the photograph she is at Kobe in 1985.

The *Pearl of Scandinavia*, built originally as the *Finlandia*, sailed the Baltic between Travemünde (in northern Germany) and Helsinki as a passenger–car ferry. Her owners were the Finnlines. In 1978–79, rebuilt for cruising in European service, on warm-weather trips to the Mediterranean, the Canaries and West Africa, she was renamed *Finnstar*. In 1981–82, she was again rebuilt for Far Eastern cruising, this time to a far more deluxe standard, for her new Pearl operators. [Built by Wärtsilä Shipyards, Helsinki, Finland, 1967. 12,456 gross tons; 505 feet long; 67 feet wide. Wärtsilä-Sulzer diesels, twin screw. Service speed 22 knots. 509 cruise passengers.]

ORIENT EXPRESS (above, bottom).

European ferry fleets and their services have expanded so that the biggest ferry is over 50,000 tons and capable of carrying 2,500 passengers. Although intended only for the short overnight trade in the Baltic between Stockholm and Helsinki, such ferries are larger than such well-known cruise ships as the *Canberra, Royal Princess* and the Carnival trio of *Holiday, Jubilee* and *Celebration*. One of the more unusual and smaller ferries plies warmer waters on the popular Eastern Mediterranean, as a combination cruise ship. She is the *Orient Express*, once operated by Britain's Sealink Ferry Group and, since 1989, in Swedish hands.

Moderate in size at 12,343 tons and carrying a maximum of 799 passengers and as many as 240 cars (in a drive-on, drive-off garage), she works a seven-day service (coordinated with the illustrious train of the same name) out of Venice to Piraeus and to Istanbul before returning via Kuşadasi, Patmos and Katákolon. From December through April, she is repositioned for seven-day sailings, from Las Palmas (in the Canary Islands) to Teneriffe, Funchal, Lanzarote, Agadir, Gran Canaria and Marrakech. She was sold in 1991. In the photograph she is at Malta.

On board, there are seven passenger decks and such amenities as indoor and outdoor pools, a gym, sauna, theater, casino, gift shop, beauty salon and barber shop. Her public rooms include the Star Lounge, Sultan's Bar, Olympic Bar, the Venice–Simplon Orient Express Restaurant and the Bosphorus Cafe. [Built by Dubigeon Normandie SA, Nantes, France, 1975. 12,343 gross tons; 499 feet long; 73 feet wide. Pielstick diesels, twin screw. Service speed 22 knots. 799 maximum passengers.]

SCANDINAVIAN SUN *(opposite, top).*

Florida-based SeaEscape Cruises has taken a series of secondhand ferries and refitted them as day cruisers, for one-day and occasional overnight cruising. They sail from such ports as Miami, Port Everglades, Port Canaveral and Tampa. Passengers come on board for early-morning departures and spend the entire day on board without having staterooms. They usually return in late evening. Gambling tends to be the most popular pastime, but there is also swimming, games, floor shows and, of course, restaurant dining. Changing facilities are available. A huge success, SeaEscape has expanded steadily from 630,000 passengers in 1987 to 700,000 a year later and 900,000 by 1989. Ships such as the *Scandinavian Sun* often set out on sell-out voyages day after day. [Built by Orenstein-Koppel Shipyard, Lübeck, West Germany, 1968. 9,902 gross tons; 441 feet long; 70 feet wide. Pielstick diesels, twin screw. Service speed 21 knots. 1,100 day passengers (200 passengers in cabin accommodation if required).]

MODERN MAINTENANCE.

The method of keeping cruise ships fit has changed over the years as well. Earlier, the ships often returned to European waters for their annual refits, entailing crossings with or without passengers and a considerable break, often in autumn, in their cruise patterns. But, as the accountants in the home offices analyzed each aspect of the operations, these overhauls were gradually eliminated. The ships no longer cross to a European yard and on-board maintenance and so-called "wet dock" repairs (made at the ship's normal berth) make dry-docking necessary only once every two years. There are the exceptions, of course, such as the *Queen Elizabeth 2*'s six-month conversion from steam-turbine machinery to diesel-electric at Bremerhaven, West Germany *(left)*. One of the busiest American yards is the Norshipco facilities at Norfolk, Virginia *(above)*, which can handle the biggest cruise liners afloat. In this aerial view, two of Carnival's cruise ships, the *Festivale* (on the left) and the *Mardi Gras* (in dry dock), are at Norfolk at the same time.

The Early Eighties: Renaissance　103

Modern Maintenance. Occasionally, there are specialized emergency repairs such as the extended work needed by Regency Cruises' *Regent Sea*, which, in December 1989, made a unusual trip northward to New York for engine work. She is shown in the former Todd Shipyards in Brooklyn, with the Lower Manhattan skyline in the background.

The Late Eighties: The Boom Continues

I N JANUARY 1988, I joined the "pre-maiden" maiden voyage of the *Sovereign of the Seas*. Sixteen hundred guests were invited aboard for a two-night "trip to nowhere." It was an exciting, eye-opening experience. More than ever, I felt I was aboard the great hotel gone to sea: a five-deck atrium for an entrance lobby, glass-bubble elevators and amenities such as 12-channel "interactive" television in every cabin. My daily exercise was just walking about the ship itself. At sailing, she had towered above the eight other cruise ships at Miami, including the mighty *Norway*.

If "big liners" seemed to be the theme of the first half of the 1980s, then "bigger still" was the theme for the second half. When she was commissioned, the 73,000-ton *Sovereign of the Seas* ranked as the fourth-largest passenger liner of all time (only the prewar *Queen Mary*, the original *Queen Elizabeth* and the *Normandie* were bigger). And if there had been any doubts about her future, her owners proudly reported that she was booked solid for her first full year of service. Two sister ships have been added, and one of them hints at yet another development: year-round cruises from San Juan, Puerto Rico.

As the cruise business, especially in North America, grows steadily each year, an even bigger trio of "mega-cruiseships" have been added by Carnival (one of the 2,600-passenger liners being for the increasingly popular short-cruise trade—overnight trips between Miami and the Bahamas). Furthermore, while some analysts predict that 80,000–90,000 tonners will be the maximum ships for overall efficiency, periodic rumors and reports continue to surround the proposed 250,000-ton *Phoenix/World City*. Extraordinary in every way, she would be the biggest passenger vessel ever created.

Two important Greek cruise operators, Royal Cruise Line and Chandris, have built their first brand-new liners during this period, and the Japanese have made a luxurious entry in Western cruising. The Norwegian-owned Seabourn Cruise Lines has commissioned twin yachts that are said to be the most expensive passenger ships yet and Royal Viking added a new flagship said to be the most luxurious of all. Finally, in an age of mergers and takeovers, there were the corporate marriages—Princess to Sitmar, and Carnival to Holland-America.

The cruise industry remains exciting and much more is yet to come.

SOVEREIGN OF THE SEAS.

The cruise industry continued to boom. A scale model *(above)*, with radio-controlled propellers and rudders, hints at the world's largest cruise ship, the *Sovereign of the Seas* of 1987. Construction began in March 1983, at the Chantiers de l'Atlantique Shipyard at St. Nazaire, France, the builders of such illustrious transatlantic liners as the *Ile de France*, both the *Frances* (1912 and 1961) and the legendary *Normandie*. This Norwegian contract represented a highly sought order in a time of otherwise badly slumped international shipbuilding. Fourteen shipyards in seven countries made bids (including the West Germans, Danes, Swedes, Finns, Japanese, the South Koreans and, of course, the French). Just before the final order was signed, the choice was between Sweden's Kockums yard, Finland's Wärtsilä and St. Nazaire. *The Sovereign of the Seas'* owners, the Oslo-based Royal Caribbean Cruise Lines, paid $183 million; the French government, wanting to keep the shipyard open and ease the 14-percent unemployment rate in the St. Nazaire area, un-

derwrote the rest, which was said to be between $40 and $90 million.

No fewer than seven tugs moved the powerless 874-foot *Sovereign of the Seas (opposite, top)* from the enormous graving dock at which the largest ships ever constructed, a quartet of 500,000-ton tankers, had also been built. As dawn broke on an April morning in 1987, a thick fog engulfed the ship. Then, as the mists cleared, her fine features began to emerge *(opposite, bottom)*. She would run trials that September and then be handed over to her owners just before Christmas. Her maiden voyage, the beginning of year-round seven-day cruises from Miami to Labadee (a private resort in Haiti), San Juan and St. Thomas, began on January 16, 1988. [Built by Chantiers de l'Atlantique, St. Nazaire, France, 1987. 73,129 gross tons; 874 feet long; 106 feet wide; 25-foot draft. Pielstick diesels, twin screw. Service speed 21 knots. 2,673 cruise-passenger maximum.]

The *Sovereign of the Seas*. Capped by one of Royal Caribbean's trademark "Viking Crowns," a cocktail lounge fitted into the funnel (seen opposite during construction and in use), the *Sovereign of the Seas* was in many ways a mighty liner reminiscent of the big transatlantic ships of bygone days. She is a ship of very impressive statistics. For example, her construction required 14,000 tons of steel—twice that of the Eiffel Tower. At completion, there were 807 miles of electrical cables (enough to stretch from Washington, D.C. to Miami), 43 miles of piping, 4 miles of corridors, 20,000 electrical

fixtures and 2,000 phones. Eighteen elevators serve both passengers and crew, and her twin bow thrusters that facilitate maneuverability during docking and undocking have the equivalent power of 44 Honda Civics. The open-air deck space is equal to 50 tennis courts or three football fields.

Shown at dock at Charlotte Amalie in St. Thomas *(above)*, the *Sovereign of the Seas* was, as expected, the most popular cruise ship of her day.

The *Sovereign of the Seas.* The ship's interiors include the exceptional five-deck high Centrum *(right, top)*, an atrium lobby that serves as the ship's entrance. Two glass-bubble elevators shuttle passengers between decks. Another space, the Windjammer Cafe *(right, bottom)*, adjacent to the ship's enormous lido deck with its twin pools, serves buffet breakfasts, luncheons and afternoon teas.

MONARCH OF THE SEAS.

Encouraged by the operating results, the performance and the profits of the *Sovereign of the Seas*, Royal Caribbean Cruise Lines decided upon two sister ships in 1989, representing a total investment of an additional $540 million. In June 1990, the two ships, with slightly higher capacities of 3,004 passengers each (the largest yet for a cruise ship), were officially named *Monarch of the Seas* and the *Majesty of the Seas*. This view shows the *Monarch* in March 1990. [Built by Chantiers de l'Atlantique, St. Nazaire, France, 1991. 74,000 gross tons; 874 feet long; 106 feet wide; 25-foot draft. Pielstick diesels, twin screw. Service speed 21 knots. 2,766 all-first-class-passenger maximum.]

CHRISTENINGS.

For christening a ship, there is no better way of assuring publicity than enlisting the services of a celebrity. When American Hawaii Cruises' *Constitution* was introduced to Hawaiian island cruise service in June 1982 she was rechristened by Princess Grace of Monaco. As film star Grace Kelly, the princess was perhaps the best-known of all passengers to have sailed on the original *Constitution*. (In spring 1956, she crossed aboard the American Export liner to Monte Carlo for her wedding to the Prince Rainier). The princess had had prior experience in christening liners. In March 1977, she had been called upon by the Cunard Line to name their *Cunard Princess* at a pierside ceremony at New York.

Of the Miami-based cruise ships, the *Norway* had been christened the *France* by Madame Charles de Gaulle in 1960. Royal Caribbean's *Song of Norway* and *Song of America* were named by superstars—actress Ingrid Bergman and opera star Beverly Sills, respectively. The mighty *Sovereign of the Seas* was christened, in January 1988, by former First Lady Rosalyn Carter. Carnival Cruise Lines' *Carnivale* is the only liner to have been christened by two queens. In her first career, in 1955, she was named by Britain's Queen Elizabeth II as the *Empress of Britain* for Canadian Pacific Steamships. In 1964, having changed hands to the Greek Line, she was rechristened as the *Queen Anna Maria* by Queen Anne Marie of Greece.

More recently there has been a trend toward film stars. Shirley Temple Black *(top, right)* named the luxurious *Seabourn Pride* at San Francisco in December 1988 and in March 1989 Audrey Hepburn *(above, left)* did the honors for Princess Cruises' *Star Princess* at Port Everglades. Mary Tyler Moore *(right)* named the Japanese liner *Crystal Harmony* at Los Angeles in July 1990 and, in September of that year, Sophia Loren christened another new Princess liner, the *Crown Princess,* at New York.

HOMERIC.

The Home Lines had long been one of the most popular cruise firms to sail out of New York, usually running on weekly trips to Nassau, later to Bermuda as well. In the mid-eighties, it sold its superb *Oceanic*, which, with 20 years of successful service, was no longer as operationally efficient or as competitive as her owner wanted her to be, and built what became the company's final ship, the *Homeric* of 1986. Then there was some rethinking. Less than two years later, in what would be the beginning of some significant mergers and buy-outs within the cruise industry, the Home Lines

and its two cruise ships (the other being the *Atlantic*) were sold for $195 million to the Holland-America Line. The Home Lines' name disappeared in the transaction and the ships changed hands, the *Homeric* going to Holland-America as the *Westerdam*, and the *Atlantic* being sold to Premier Cruise Lines and thereafter being advertised as the *Starship Atlantic*. This view shows the *Homeric* being launched on September 28, 1985. [Built by Meyerwerft Shipyards, Papenburg, West Germany, 1986. 42,092 gross tons; 669 feet long; 95 feet wide. Burmeister & Wain–type diesels, twin screw. Service speed 22.5 knots. 1,030 cruise passengers.]

WESTERDAM.

In November 1988, soon after the *Homeric* was transferred to Holland-America and made her first sailing *(opposite)* from Port Everglades as the *Westerdam*, Holland-America Line was bought out for $625 million by Carnival Cruise Lines. This included not only the four Dutch cruise ships (the *Rotterdam*, *Nieuw Amsterdam* and *Noordam* being the others), but Windstar Sail Cruises and Westours as well, making Carnival the biggest cruise owner-operator anywhere.

Among the first decisions within the newly merged organization (although Carnival and Holland-America kept separate identities) was to lengthen the *Westerdam*, the largest ship of her kind ever so treated. The expansion involved the insertion of a 130-foot section into the ship, increasing her size from 42,000 to over 53,000 tons. Her lower-berth capacity has increased from 1,030 to 1,476 (upperberth offering additional accommodations). The length of the ship has increased from 668 to 798 feet, making her the largest ship ever owned by the Holland-America Line.

The *Westerdam* was returned to her builders, the Meyer Werft Shipyards, where she had been constructed three years before. Her transformation took from October 1989 until the following March. The photographs show the ship, under the largest enclosed shed in the world, being prepared for lengthening *(right)* and then her reintroduction to cruise service at New York *(above)*.

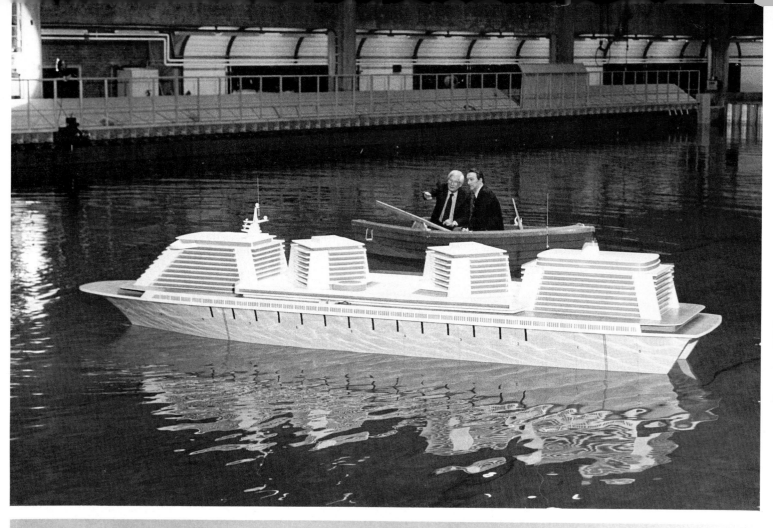

PHOENIX–WORLD CITY (opposite, top).

Design firms were kept busy in the eighties with newer, larger and certainly more ambitious cruise-ship projects, the most noteworthy being the *Phoenix* Project, which was later renamed *World City*. Statistically, she would be the largest passenger vessel ever built: 250,000 gross tons, 1,246 feet long, 170 feet wide and with quarters for 5,200 passengers and 1,850 crew. Although no firm building had been scheduled at the time of writing, it has been planned that she would be created by four separate shipyards and then joined together by the largest. Her cost, said to require the assistance of nearly 100 international banks, would be approximately $1 billion. She would be owned and operated by the World City Corporation. The scheme is headed by Knut Kloster, the Norwegian shipper who had been head of the Kloster Group, the owners of the Norwegian Cruise and Royal Viking lines. According to tentative plans, she would operate about half the year in European waters and the other half in the Caribbean, with a base at Port Canaveral in Florida.

The ship is designed to accommodate her passengers in three hotel-like towers (the original model, seen here, contained four), each a resort separate unto itself. Massive portals in the stern of the vessel would open to reveal a large marina within the ship. Four day cruisers, each with a capacity of 400, would dock inside the ship and would shuttle within a 50-mile radius. Other facilities would include village squares, a recreation of "Downtown U.S.A.," Rendezvous Plaza, Main Street, galleries, museums, a house of worship, tropical gardens, a sports arena, sidewalk cafés, nightclubs, a 2,500-seat movie theater, discos, several pools, a 100,000-volume library, a 1,500-seat conference center, a brokerage office, an arts complex, at least a dozen restaurants and an entire shopping center.

PRINCESS CRUISES (opposite, bottom; above; overleaf).

In the summer of 1988, in another unexpected takeover, British-owned Princess Cruises acquired the Monte Carlo–based Sitmar Cruises. This included four existing ships (one of which, the *Fairwind*, was the first to change over to Princess colors and adopt a new name, *Dawn Princess*—seen opposite, bottom, in September 1988). Sitmar Cruises disappeared and the Princess fleet increased to eight liners. [Built by John Brown & Company Limited, Clydebank, Scotland, 1957. 21,989 gross tons; 608 feet long; 80 feet wide. Steam turbines, twin screw. Service speed 19 knots. 925 cruise passengers.]

Princess also acquired a trio of "newbuildings" that had been underway with Sitmar. The French-built *Fairmajesty* was redubbed *Star Princess* prior to her completion in March 1989. She is shown (*overleaf*) arriving at Vancouver's Canada Place Terminal in the following June. [Built by Chantiers de l'Atlantique, St. Nazaire, France, 1989. 62,500 gross tons; 804 feet long; 102 feet wide. Burmeister & Wain–type diesels, twin screw. Service speed 21 knots. 1,470 cruise passengers (1,700 maximum berths).]

The *Star Princess* was followed by two even larger sister ships, the *Crown Princess* (shown above fitting out at Monfalcone, Italy, in October 1989) and her twin, the *Regal Princess*. The former was added to the Princess fleet in June 1990; the latter in the fall of 1991. [*Crown Princess:* built by Fincantieri Shipyards, Monfalcone, Italy, 1990. 70,000 gross tons; 804 feet long; 105 feet wide. Diesels, twin screw. Service speed 19.5 knots. 1,600 cruise passengers.]

Princess Cruises, one of the leaders of the international cruise industry, has been particularly noteworthy with its specialty-theme cruises. Among cruises offered in the late eighties were: Women of Distinction, Salute to the Lawrence Welk Show, Olympic Superstars, Chocolate Celebration, Rock 'n' Roll, Politicians & the Media, Salute to Football, Golden Age of Television, Baseball Hall of Fame, Authors, Salute to *Sixty Minutes* (a television news program), Salute to the Los Angeles Dodgers and even a Born to Shop cruise.

SEABOURN PRIDE.

The luxury-cruise business continued to expand, with ships such as the *Seabourn Pride (opposite, top)* and *Seabourn Spirit*. They are operated on international schedules by the Norwegian-owned, San Francisco–based Seabourn Cruise Lines. Patterned after large luxury yachts and the two Sea Goddess cruise yachts, they have nine passenger decks but carry just over 200 passengers. Views of the *Seabourn Pride* give an idea of her facilities. The gourmet restaurant *(above)* has open seating throughout the day (as the descriptive literature suggests, "dine when and with whom you please at each and every meal"). All the cabins (one is shown opposite, bottom) are suites, measuring an impressive 277 square feet and offering such amenities as five-foot-high windows, walk-in closets, entertainment units, bars and marble baths. [Built by Seebeckwerft A/G, Bremerhaven, West Germany, 1988. 8,200 gross tons; 439 feet long; 63 feet wide. Diesels, twin screw. Service speed 19 knots. 212 cruise passengers.]

GREEK ADDITIONS.
Greek shipowners, long known to be interested in converting secondhand passenger-ship tonnage, added new ships as well in the late eighties. Both Royal Cruise Lines and Chandris Cruises added their first brand-new ships, both shown arriving at New York for the first time. The *Crown Odyssey* of Royal Cruise *(above)* is shown off Lower Manhattan in September 1988; the Chandris *Horizon (opposite)* is seen off the Statue of Liberty in May 1990. [*Crown*

Odyssey: built by Meyer Werft Shipyards, Papenburg, West Germany, 1988. 34,242 gross tons; 614 feet long; 92 feet wide. Diesels, twin screw. Service speed 21 knots. 1,052 cruise passengers. *Horizon:* built by Meyer Werft Shipyards, Papenburg, West Germany, 1990. 46,811 gross tons; 682 feet long; 95 feet wide. Diesels, twin screw. Service speed 21.5 knots. 1,354 cruise passengers (1,677-passenger maximum).]

ROYAL VIKING SUN (opposite, top).

The luxurious Royal Viking Line commissioned a fourth and larger addition to its original trio of the early seventies. Named *Royal Viking Sun*, she is shown arriving at New York in August 1989, together with the *Royal Viking Star* (right). The *Sun*, used on worldwide cruise schedules, was then on a series of two-week cruises to the St. Lawrence River, the Canadian Maritimes and New England; the *Star* was plying a weekly service of cruises between New York and Bermuda. Pleased with its new ship, Royal Viking was especially delighted when one noted travel publication named the *Sun* the most luxurious liner afloat in 1989–90. [Built by Wärtsilä Shipyards, Turku, Finland, 1988. 37,845 gross tons; 670 feet long; 95 feet wide. Wärtsilä-Sulzer diesels, twin screw. Service speed 21.5 knots. 760 cruise passengers.]

CRYSTAL HARMONY (opposite, bottom).

By the late eighties, the Japanese had taken a strong interest in cruising, particularly in the North American and European luxury trades. The N.Y.K. Line, the biggest shipping company in the world, decided to invest $1 billion in three large liners. Operated by Los Angeles–based Crystal Cruises and flying the Bahamian flag, first of these, the *Crystal Harmony*, was delivered in the spring 90. She is staffed by Norwegian officers and an international staff. Japanese presence was kept at a minimum. Used initially on the West Coast–Alaska service and then in the Caribbean, ship was scheduled to be transferred to European waters in 992. She is seen here in Nagasaki Harbor.

The *Crystal Harmony*'s accommodations emphasize spaciousness: She carries only 960 maximum passengers. Her top accommodations, the so-called "Crystal Penthouses," have the largest verandas ever to put to sea, measuring a total of 948 square feet. Other verandas are fitted to half of all her cabins, all of which have sitting areas,

showers and bathtubs, oversized closets, interactive television and VCR units, twin beds that are convertible to queen size or king size, mini-refrigerators and bathroom amenities that include hair dryers, robes and make-up mirrors.

The extensive public areas include a two-story atrium, an "Avenue of the Stars" shopping arcade, a "Caesar's Palace at Sea" casino, a piano bar, a domed observation lounge with triple-level seating and a 270-degree view, a sloped-seating main lounge, several special-purpose lounges and a wine bar. Dining facilities are offered in the main dining room, a grill room and an Oriental specialty restaurant. [Built by Mitsubishi Heavy Industries Shipyard, Nagasaki, Japan, 1990. 49,400 gross tons; 791 feet long; 97 feet wide; 24-foot draft. Mitsubishi diesels, twin screw. Service speed 22 knots. 960 cruise passengers.]

WINDSTAR CRUISES (above).

Another form of cruising was offered by the Windstar trio, the first of which was commissioned in the fall of 1986. The large sails, which are controlled by computerized machinery and use little manpower, give passengers the "sail experience" in an otherwise conventional vessel. The sailing, which accounts for about half the entire voyage time, is done during daylight hours in tranquil waters. The ships, with luxurious quarters, are named *Wind Star*, *Wind Song* (shown here off Tahiti) and *Wind Spirit*, and sail on week-long itineraries: the Caribbean, South Pacific, western Mediterranean and the Greek isles. A single season in Alaskan waters proved unsuccessful—they are warm-weather ships. [*Wind Song*: built by Ateliers et Chantiers du Havre, Le Havre, France, 1987. 5,307 gross tons; 440 feet long; 52 feet wide. Diesels (auxiliary to sail power), twin screw. Service speed 12 knots maximum. 160 cruise-passenger maximum.]

A NEW CARNIVAL TRIO (above).

As the North American cruise industry reached a $5 billion annual level in 1990, the short-cruise industry—those three- and four-day trips, most between Florida and the nearby Bahamas—was the fastest-growing segment of the entire business. Between 1980 and 1990, volume had increased by 200 percent. It was for this trade that the acute Carnival Cruise Lines directed the first of its next "megaliner" trio—the 70,000-ton *Fantasy*, shown at Miami, which was delivered in the winter of 1990. She is one of the largest cruise ships ever built and two sister ships, the *Ecstasy* and the *Sensation*, are planned for the Caribbean markets.

The *Fantasy* and her sisters are the bigger versions of the earlier *Holiday* class, built in the mid-eighties. Everything seems to be on a larger, "glitzier" scale. The six-deck-high atrium, for example, is the largest of its kind yet built in a ship. Called the Grand Spectrum, it is highlighted by a glass skylight that constantly changes color and the room's ambience through a computerized lighting system. In fact, the ship is marked by light; there are over 20 miles of neon alone in the ship's public spaces. One of her main public areas is named Century Boulevard, the casino is the largest yet placed on board a cruise ship and the health center–spa is also the biggest of its kind.

The *Fantasy* was constructed during hard economic times for many shipbuilders. Just before her completion, Wärtsilä, Finland's largest single source of foreign currency and the employer of 6,500 people, went into bankruptcy. Their losses of $99 million in 1987 rose to $148 million a year later. The yard went into reorganization and completed the *Ecstasy*, but with considerable cost overruns (from $225 million to perhaps as much as $275 million). Eventually, the yard received the order for the third ship, the *Sensation*. [Built by Wärtsilä Shipyards, Helsinki, Finland, 1990. 70,367 gross tons; 860 feet long; 102 feet wide; 25-foot draft. Sulzer diesels, twin screw. Service speed 21 knots. 2,600 cruise passengers.]

THE GROWTH OF CRUISING (opposite; overleaf).

There were a record 3.5 million cruise passengers in 1989 and further growth is predicted. Fourteen new passenger ships were added to the international schedules a year later and still more were on the drawing boards for construction well into the 1990s. Yet only five percent of all potential cruise travelers have actually taken a cruise. Many industry analysts see television advertising as a major form of recruitment for winning over more vacationers. In the late eighties, television was taking larger shares of advertising budgets: Carnival was the highest, with annual billings of $14.4 million; Royal Caribbean followed at $12.1 million, Norwegian Cruise at $8.6 million and Holland America at $7.9 million. More ships are enjoying 100 percent occupancy rates.

The busiest embarkation/disembarkation ports for 1990 were Miami (3.1 million passengers and estimating 4 million by 2000), Port Everglades (1.75 million), Port Canaveral (913,000), Los Angeles (600,000), Vancouver (331,000) and New York (330,000). The busiest cruise ports, all of them in the Caribbean area, were S Thomas (with 994,000 cruise visitors), Nassau (947,000), San J (800,000), Freeport (780,000) and St. Maarten (500,000).

Overall, the cruise industry offers choices of destinatio itineraries and provides a well-priced, relaxing vacation. ports such as Vancouver (shown opposite, bottom, with the *Princess*, *Sea Goddess II* and *Noordam* at berth) and New York (se opposite, top, with the outbound *Norway* passing the inbound *Rotterdam*) offer seasonal cruise services, the busier ports such as Miami (seen overleaf with nine liners at dock: *Bohème, Nordic Prince, Song of Norway, Sun Viking, Skyward, Norway, Rhapsody, Festivale* and *Caribe*) offer year-round services. It is a very busy industry.

Alphabetical List of Ships Illustrated

The pages listed are those containing text references. Some ships bore several names during their careers; the reference is to the name of the ship as shown in the photograph.